LESLEY RILEY

Photo Memory Quilts

• THE ULTIMATE GUIDE TO •

Contemporary Heirloom Quilts to Showcase Ancestry, History & Treasured Times

C&T PUBLISHING
Another Maker Inspired!

Text and photography copyright © 2023 by Lesley Riley

Photography and artwork copyright © 2023 by C&T Publishing, Inc.

Publisher: Amy Barrett-Daffin

Creative Director: Gailen Runge

Senior Editor: Roxane Cerda

Editor: Liz Aneloski

Technical Editor: Helen Frost

Cover/Book Designer: April Mostek

Production Coordinator: Tim Manibusan

Photography Coordinator: Lauren Herberg

Photography Assistant: Rachel Ackley

Front cover photography: Top row by Lauren Herberg for C&T Publishing, middle row by Kyle Gula, bottom row by Lesley Riley

Photography by Lesley Riley, unless otherwise noted

Published by C&T Publishing, Inc., P.O. Box 1456, Lafayette, CA 94549

Attention Teachers: C&T Publishing, Inc., encourages the use of our books as texts for teaching. You can find lesson plans for many of our titles at ctpub.com or contact us at ctinfo@ctpub.com.

We take great care to ensure that the information included in our products is accurate and presented in good faith, but no warranty is provided, nor are results guaranteed. Having no control over the choices of materials or procedures used, neither the author nor C&T Publishing, Inc., shall have any liability to any person or entity with respect to any loss or damage caused directly or indirectly by the information contained in this book. For your convenience, we post an up-to-date listing of corrections on our website (ctpub.com). If a correction is not already noted, please contact our customer service department at ctinfo@ctpub.com or P.O. Box 1456, Lafayette, CA 94549.

Trademark (™) and registered trademark (®) names are used throughout this book. Rather than use the symbols with every occurrence of a trademark or registered trademark name, we are using the names only in the editorial fashion and to the benefit of the owner, with no intention of infringement.

Library of Congress Cataloging-in-Publication Data

Names: Riley, Lesley, 1952- author.

Title: Photo memory quilts : the ultimate guide to contemporary heirloom

quilts to showcase ancestry, history & treasured times / Lesley Riley.

Description: Lafayette, CA : C&T Publishing, Inc., [2023] | Summary:

"Quilters and sewists of all experience levels will learn how to

beautifully incorporate treasured photographs into a visual heirloom to

be displayed and handed down. Lesley walks readers through all aspects

of using photos for quilting including sourcing photos, custom printing,

vintage photo manipulation, fabric selection, vintage textiles, and

more"-- Provided by publisher.

Identifiers: LCCN 2022047167 | ISBN 9781644031971 (trade paperback) | ISBN

9781644031988 (ebook)

Subjects: LCSH: Quilts--Patterns. | Quilts--Themes, motives. | Photographs on cloth.

Classification: LCC TT835 .R5388 2023 | DDC 746.46--dc23/eng/20221013

LC record available at https://lccn.loc.gov/2022047167

Printed in China

10 9 8 7 6 5 4 3 2 1

Dedication

Photo by Buddy Riley

Selecting an image, "We pluck that moment out of life and isolate it so that it can be examined."
— JEAN RAY LAURY —

Jean Ray Laury was my first quilt teacher via her 1970 book, *Quilts and Coverlets: A Contemporary Approach*, a book my mother purchased when she was 45—about the same age I was when I rediscovered quilting and began the journey that has led to this book. But it was Laury's 1977 book, *The Creative Woman's Getting-It-All-Together at Home Handbook*, that made my art-life possible. It kept me focused and was my lifeline to other creative women at a time when I knew none.

Fast-forward 30-plus years. Imagine my surprise when she was a student in a class I was teaching for the Fresno Fiber-Arts Guild. Jean—in *my* class? It made me realize that I really did have something to offer to the quilt world.

It all came full circle when I invited her to collaborate on a group project my dear friend Christine Adams and I were spearheading, titled Women of Influence. Not only did Laury say yes, but she secured an exhibit space at the Fresno Art Museum for it and invited us to her home for dinner when we traveled to see the show and teach a workshop there.

Laury believed that "a great quilt exists when it relies on … the principles of art that make any piece of visual work look great. … Art has less to do with the material used than with the perceptive and expressive abilities of the individual."

"While Laury was recognized internationally as a pioneer of the art quilt movement, her life mission was simply to inspire others to see the greatness and artistic abilities within themselves" (Wikipedia). I'm carrying the torch, Jean.

This book is dedicated to her memory.

Acknowledgments

A thank-you isn't enough to say how grateful I am for the generosity, kindness, and participation of the 21 contributing artists who enrich this book with their time and talents. You all make this a better book, for sure. I am so happy that I could share your work with my readers.

I am honored and grateful that the team at C&T put their faith in me again for yet another book. So much has changed since the first one we did together in 2009. We have traveled together from analog to digital and everything in between with grace, support, and understanding.

To my sister, Katie Jackson, who is always my first reader, advisor, and eagle eye. Many thanks to Delmar Danner of Danner's BERNINA Shoppe and Michelle Umlauf for helping me meet my deadline.

Last, but never, ever the least, thank you to my ever-growing family and my patient, understanding husband. He takes very good care of me. What a blessing to have the loving support of 28 cheerleaders. You mean everything to me.

Contents

PROJECTS
64

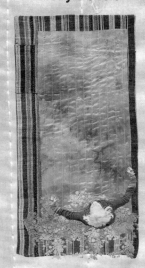

Introduction

Art is the technique of communication. The image is the
most complete technique of all communication.
— CLAES OLDENBURG —

Memory is a personal, ethereal, formless thing, drifting like clouds in our heads, heart, and soul. Visual memory is something recalled and seen in your mind's eye—actual events, people, places, and things. Photos, trinkets, letters, ephemera, textiles, and more are meaningful objects connected to a memory. Most important, a memory is a story. Search through those boxes, scrapbooks, and envelopes. Ransack the cupboards, drawers, and attic. Gather, reminisce, daydream, remember. All these memories you have been holding onto for so long have been waiting for this moment to arrive.

Let's make a memory quilt! Are you ready to begin?

Within these pages, you will discover how to get inspired, develop your ideas, and learn a variety of methods and techniques to turn your vision into reality. We will start by getting clear on the who, what, why, or where of your memory quilt. I will walk you through the how and where of gathering or finding photos, repairing or enhancing them, and turning the blah into beautiful through the creative use of apps. I will share all my thoughts and know-how on fabric and how it relates to and enhances storytelling.

Composition and design can make or break a memory quilt, so you'll get a primer (or refresher) on these key elements and principles. You will see how all of this comes together when I detail and share the start-to-finish steps on eight different memory quilts. A gallery of photo memory quilts by eighteen contributing artists will further in-

Family Garden, 19″ × 19″

Collage memory quilt with original gem tintypes
and altered Lutradur flowers

spire your own creative expression. All of the outstanding quilters in this book were chosen because I knew they could, and would, inspire you as you embark on your own approach, literally taking your memories into your own hands.

My Story

I fell in love with fabric and quilting over 50 years ago and have been making photo memory quilts for over 20 years. My creative ideas and dreams were unleashed when I purchased my first inkjet printer around the year 2000. From the very beginning, I was (and still am) inspired by old photographs and the stories, real or imagined, behind them. At the same time, I was completing my degree in women's studies and came to the realization that the women in the photos I had been collecting for 30 years were the foundation and inspiration for the stories I wanted to tell. Their anonymous faces represented every woman and became the starting point and means to illustrate the stories, memories, and concepts I wanted to share, including my own.

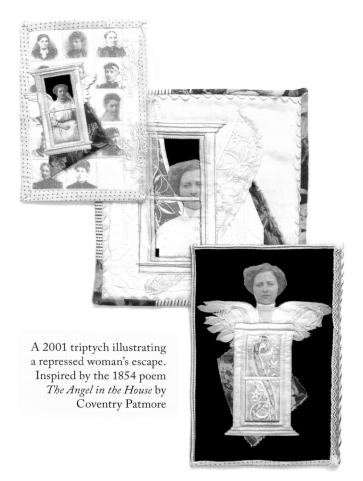

A 2001 triptych illustrating a repressed woman's escape. Inspired by the 1854 poem *The Angel in the House* by Coventry Patmore

Developing the triptych plan and fabrics in my journal

I use textiles, old and new, and found or saved materials to connect to people, places, things, and events that spark interest and meaning for me. I tell visual stories. They are my personal response to history. A memory, no matter how recent, is history—whether it is personal, family, community, local, national, or universal—that is shared or passed down through the ages. A quilt made now will become an even more powerful memory in the years to come. Think of the future impact of the recent Covid and social justice quilts, or the flood of memories my 2001 quilt unleashed when I compared it with my life today—my everlasting memory of a moment in time.

The Apron, 20˝ × 30˝

Made in 2001, this quilt top is now a precious remembrance of my past conflict
between the life I created versus the creative life I desired.

Storytelling with fabric has been my passion for many years, and a natural extension of my love of reading and writing. Stories are comprised of fragments of fact and memory. Like a quilt, these fragments are stitched together to create and preserve your stories and history. By using textiles to bring our memories out of our heart and soul and into the world, we create something that can be universally understood and related to. Luckily for us, even a single piece, pattern, color, or texture of fabric can conjure up many memories.

Quilts and antique or vintage textiles are artifacts. They serve as historical and collective evidence. Old and new textiles, combined with the modern materials and photography methods that you will use to preserve your memory quilt, will one day become an heirloom and part of our material culture. What you make, matters.

My style is a mix of classic and modern, often with a graphic quality—the old reframed with a modern vibe. I make old things new so that they are seen in a new light, with fresh eyes. I offer many styles and ideas for you in this book. It may sometimes seem that every work of mine was made by a different person! Look closely; there is coherence. My voice is present in them all.

Take note of the ideas and techniques that resonate with you. You learn best not just by doing the steps and processes I share in this book, but by experimenting for yourself. There is no one "right" way to create your memory quilt. Always approach your work with a "Why not?" or "What if?" attitude. In fact, I encourage it! Think of this book as your starting point and idea generator.

Memory Subjects

Memories are made of fleeting bits and scraps, visual or felt, sometimes altered (intentionally or not), tucked away in a place you return to in quiet reverie. A memory can be small and personal, existing only in your head, or as large and all-encompassing as an international event. No matter the size, it is still yours, your personal memory of something just you—or the world and every relationship in between—might share. It will always be personal and your story to tell (or not, more about that later). Your memory, in the form of your quilt, will always be from your hands and through your eyes, heart, and soul—an expression of self.

Storyboard development of a personal memory quilt idea, inspired by an old book illustration. Original book page was enlarged, printed on TAP Transfer Artist Paper, hand colored, and transferred to bleached muslin.

Your photo memory quilt can be inspired by a photo or begin with an object, recollection, remembrance, or reminiscence. It is going to be about something you want to remember, celebrate, honor, share, and treasure. This may include one or all of the following:

PEOPLE—family and genealogy, heroes, strangers from photos with made-up stories

PLACES—home; neighborhood; towns, cities, and countries visited; secret rooms, secret gardens; indoors and out

THINGS—cyanotypes; historic, meaningful, or collected objects; nature; abstract ideas

EVENTS—birth, death; graduations, weddings, reunions, holidays; political, life-changing, world-changing

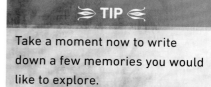

≫ TIP ≪

Take a moment now to write down a few memories you would like to explore.

Just the Facts Versus Wild Imagination

Personal or shared (with family, community, town, country, world), your telling, or in this case, showing, of this memory is your personal, first-person story. Just as we have many different ways available to us to tell a story, there are several ways you can approach your memory quilt.

NEWS REPORT—narrow scope with just the facts, ma'am

DOCUMENTARY—educational true story, straightforward but from your point of view

BASED ON A TRUE STORY—told with artistic license and imagination

EMBELLISHED REALITY—inspired by an actual person, place, or thing, but veering from actual or factual events

TOTALLY FICTION—made up, from a dream, wishful thinking, fantasy, abstraction

Fading Memory, 13″ × 8″, by Gina Louthian-Stanley

As you can see, a memory quilt can be created in a variety of ways. You're in charge of how much or how little you want to reveal. Some memories are private, sacred, painful, or secret, and you want to express them in a memory quilt but you don't want others to know some part or all of it. There are several techniques and ways to create this visual memory while obscuring the details. Consider abstracted images, mysterious imagery, or blurred photos in combination with the elements and principles of design to create shapes, lines, and forms that hold meaning or indicate your feelings, yet need not be explained.

Photograph Rules, Sources & Research

Photographs are our silent records of the past, of moments frozen in time. Photos inspire stories. Stories inspire ideas. Ideas inspire art. You can create a memory quilt without photos, but this is a book about photo memory quilts, so let's talk a bit about photos.

A collector of old photos since I was in my twenties, I was instinctively drawn in by certain images, like a moth to a flame, not even knowing why. I just had to have them. At the time I had no use for them, but still, I collected. Thirty years later, it all fell into place. Hundreds of fragments and quilts later, my photo passion still drives me. My quilts just don't feel complete without a photo.

Vintage photos from my collection

Perhaps you, too, have a collection of old photos. You may be the lucky bearer of family photos passed down to you or shared with a sibling. More recent photos from your childhood and pre-cell phone days may be hiding out in a photo book, box, or drawer, along with other mementos and ephemera too precious or meaningful to dispose of. And it is a safe bet to say you have dozens, hundreds, or even thousands of digital photos on your phone or computer.

You can still find old photos for sale in antique shops, at estate sales, and online. They are often referred to as "instant ancestors." There's just something captivating about an old photo, and the technology that created it, that our slick digital photos don't have—even if the old photo needs some work.

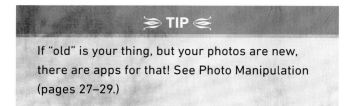

≽ TIP ≼

If "old" is your thing, but your photos are new, there are apps for that! See Photo Manipulation (pages 27–29.)

One of the prime benefits of living in the digital age is that there is a seemingly unending supply of free and copyright-free photos at your fingertips. More become available every day, as archives and museums worldwide digitize their collections. This vast supply of photographs and images enables you to tell stories and augment memories, not only of a personal nature, but of people, places, history, nature, science, art, artists, events, and more. The public domain was designed to collect, preserve, and teach us about our past, making our cultural history more accessible to the population, not just in the United States, but in many other countries as well.

Photograph circa 1900. Image courtesy of State Library, Victoria, Australia. *Photographer unknown*

Public Domain Images

An image passes into the public domain when the copyright has expired or it was never copyrighted (see note below). A photograph or illustration enters the public domain 70 years after the death of its creator unless the copyright is renewed by the creator's heirs.

NOTE ℗ *As of January 1, 1978, under United States copyright law, a work is automatically protected by copyright when it is created. You need to register your copyright if you feel that there may be a need to take legal action to protect it in the future. For more information, refer to the U.S. Copyright Office or your national copyright office.*

Sojourner Truth's copyrighted (expired) portrait

All images in the U.S. Government Image Collections are in the public domain. The United States has copyright relations with most countries throughout the world, and as a result of these agreements, countries honor each other's citizens' copyrights. However, the United States does not have such copyright relationships with every country. If you are using images from collections held outside of the United States, refer to the copyright and use restrictions information provided on the photo source's website or to U.S. Copyright Office Circular 38A, *International Copyright Relations of the United States*. Remember, copyright laws protect your work, too.

Artists of all kinds—writers, musicians, filmmakers, painters—rely on the public domain. *Romeo and Juliet* inspired *West Side Story*; Disney drew from the Brothers Grimm and Hans Christian Anderson. The public domain feeds creativity.

All images that are in the public domain may be used freely, restored, digitized, and published without attribution.

Sojourner Truth, abolitionist and women's rights activist, filed for a copyright in 1864 for a photograph of herself that she had engraved with her words, "I sell the Shadow to Support the Substance. Sojourner Truth," using the 1802 law enacted by Congress that anyone "who shall invent and design, engrave, etch or work, or from his own works and inventions, shall cause to be designed and engraved, etched or worked, any historical or other print or prints, shall have the sole right and liberty of printing, re-printing, publishing and vending such print or prints …." By registering her engraved photograph, Truth was able to make a living by speaking and selling her image.

Restricted Use

Another group of photos that are under copyright is available to you through the Creative Commons, a global, nonprofit network that offers an internationally recognized system of alternatives to full copyright. The works available are copyrighted, but under copyright law, copyright owners can choose to license their work under more generous terms than standard copyright.

This means that you may be able to use a photo as long as you comply with certain rules or restrictions, that is, give credit to the creator, use it for noncommercial purposes, and/or other minor restrictions. Creative Commons has created a set of symbols that accompany restricted use. They are displayed with any restricted-use photo to inform you of the restrictions.

Copyright Yes, No & Maybe

I never know where my art will appear, so I always make the effort to ensure that any photograph, or any photo of a painting or drawing, that I use is copyright free, in the public domain, or used with permission of the creator or owner. The copyright owner may not be the creator of the work, and therefore does not have copyright privileges, but when the image is in their collection, it is always a best practice to ask permission, especially since the copyrighted photo you see online was likely taken by the institution or owner of the uncopyrighted image and therefore is a copyrighted *photograph* of the original.

It never hurts to ask to use an image if you can locate its source, copyrighted or not. Almost every institution will have a link to its permissions department on its website. There will be a contact link or a form to submit outlining your intended use. Personal and educational use is usually free or carries a small fee. I have also asked private collectors who have copyrighted their photograph of an uncopyrighted image if I may use their image. I have not been turned down once they know my purpose and intended use of the image. Often, they will have a higher-resolution image they will share with me as well.

A page from Emily Dickinson's *Herbarium* © President and Fellows of Harvard University. Used with permission.

When in doubt, leave it out. It's rare, but sometimes there isn't enough information to ascertain whether an image is in the public domain and/or copyright free. If, after you have done your due diligence, and you cannot verify the status, then be safe and find something else to use.

Just Ask

Just Ask

A copyright notice does not always equate to *not* being able to use an image, especially when it is on a photo-sharing site such as Flickr. In many instances, all you need to do is contact the person who copyrighted it, let them know why and how you would use the image, and ask for permission. This especially applies to antique and vintage images that people have photographed and posted. If the person gives you permission, keep a record of it for your protection.

Downloads & Screenshots

You've found a photo online you can use. Now what? Many sites will provide a download link on the image page. Some sites offer the option of downloading in different resolutions. The higher the resolution, the more detail (in the form of pixels) you will have to work with and the larger you can potentially print the image. Keep in mind, it will also take up more space on your computer or tablet.

If the download is not automatic:

Right-click on a PC

Control/right-click (together) on a Mac

You will be asked how and where to save the image. Saving the image as a JPG file is the usual choice. I've learned over the years to create a folder for each project and save my downloaded images there.

A screenshot is an easy way to capture a public domain or copyright-free image from your screen. I use printed screenshots in the early stages of planning my work, but the size and resolution are usually not large enough for a print-quality image. One workaround is to enlarge the image on your screen before taking the screenshot.

⋙ TIP ⋘

Enlarge the screen image before you take a screenshot by holding down the *Command* key and tapping the + key on a Mac or PC. Use the *dash/minus* key to reduce the screen back down.

My Best-Kept Secret

Sometimes I fall in love with a vintage or antique image and discover that I must pay to acquire the rights to use it, even if it's for personal one-time use. Here's the secret—many of the old images you find for sale online are in the public domain. Yes, you can pay someone for their copyrighted image, the one resulting from all the work they've done to edit, repair, and clean up the image, or you can search for the same image in the public domain and do that work yourself. It only takes a minute to look, thanks to a reverse image search engine. I use TinEye.com.

TinEye shows you all the places where the image is found online. Look to see if there is one found in a public domain source as opposed to a blog or advertisement (which is not always a legal or permission-based use). Check the pixel size of the image, too. You always want the largest file available for the best enlargement and printing options. Follow the link to that source and download the public domain image. See Resources (page 127) for lists of photo and research sources.

Photo Repair & Enhancing

Mom and Dad, colorized with an app

NOTE ↻ *I use an iPhone, so my instructions will be based on iPhone functions and screens. Most smartphones will have all of the same functionality but perhaps with different names or locations in and on the screen of the photo-editing area. It should be easy to equate your screen with what is presented here.*

You've chosen your photo(s). Now it is time to polish them up enough to be quilt worthy. The good news is that, in most instances, it can all be done using the photo editing and other applications on your smartphone or tablet. You've had the power in your hands all along!

Unfortunately, not everyone back in the day was a skilled photographer, and not every old photo is in perfect condition. You may have blurs, cracks, scratches, dust, yellowing, fading, and more to deal with. Modern technology comes to the rescue—sometimes with just a tap or two on your device. The techniques and processes I use may seem confusing, scary, or difficult at first, but with practice, you can make almost any photo shine.

To prepare your smartphone or tablet for optimum photo taking, go to *Settings > Photos*. Newer devices automatically take high-resolution photos and will not display any resolution options. If you have an older device, you may see options for taking and saving high- and low-resolution photos. Choose *high*.

How to Photograph a Photograph

NOTE ℗ *The photographs in this section show my camera in the vertical position with the icons and controls at the bottom. If you are using your device in the horizontal mode, the icons and controls will be on the side of your screen.*

Camera screen with grid and crosshairs

If you have an actual photo, versus one you have downloaded from the internet or taken on your device, the first thing you need to do is take a photo of it. I no longer scan my photos as I have found my iPhone does a better job.

1. Inspect the photo for any dust or debris and gently remove it with a dust-free cloth.

2. Natural daylight is best. Turn off overhead or table lamps to avoid shadows, glare, and color casts. Place your photo on a clean white surface on a table top. (I use a piece of foam core.) Tack down any curled edges on the photo. (I use a rolled piece of tape.)

3. Open the *camera* function and turn off the *flash* and *HDR* settings. (The High Dynamic Range camera setting comes in handy when you have trouble balancing a photo's light, i.e., due to backlighting or low lighting, and is not applicable here.)

4. Frame the photo on the screen, allowing for some of the white background to remain. You will be cropping later. If the image appears blurry, move the camera farther back so it can focus.

5. Note the grid and crosshairs located in the center. These assist you in taking a photo straight-on, without any skew in perspective. Align the yellow and white crosshairs so they merge into one yellow crosshair.

6. On the screen, tap on the face or desired focal point. and the camera will focus on it. To lock the focal point, tap and hold on your focal point until you see an *AE/AF Lock* banner appear at the top of the screen.

7. With the focal point locked, align the crosshairs again, hold steady, and take the photo.

If you are not happy with the photo, make any improvements necessary and reshoot, or you can make any needed changes in the next step, editing.

RESIZING PHOTOGRAPHS

Before you move on to editing your photos, you need to check the file size of the images you'll be using in your quilt. Chances are that the ones you have photographed yourself are the right size to work with. But, photos and screenshots you take from the internet should always be checked to ensure that there are enough pixels available at the right resolution to print a sharp, non-pixelated image at the size you need. This step will avoid future disappointment.

For the iPhone operating system, IOS, select the photo, and tap the *i* in the circle icon at the bottom of the phone. This will display the pixels. Android users may find this information by tapping the three dots or lines on the screen and selecting *Details*.

Size matters! A high-resolution image, 300 dots per inch (dpi) is necessary for good-quality printing. This is the resolution of most printers. To determine how to print your image in high resolution (300 dpi), use the inches of your image and multiply both the width and the height by 300. That means in order to create a sharp, high-res 8″ × 8″ image on a printer set to 300 dpi, you will need a minimum of 2,400 × 2,400 pixels available.

Photo Terms & Math

All digital images are composed of pixels. Zoom in on any image and you will see the actual pixels it is composed of. Photo printing terms are based on the number of pixels in an image. Digital photos and photo printing can be confusing when you do not understand the lingo or terms used when talking about print-ready photos. There are just three basic things you need to be aware of to get the size and quality you need.

dpi Versus Resolution

As ("dots per inch") implies, *dpi* is primarily a *printing* term for how many dots of ink per inch the printer will spray on the paper or printing surface. *Resolution* is the number of pixels in a digital image, stated in millions of pixels aka *megapixels*. Newer devices take photos at a very high resolution offering more megapixels. The more MP your device has, the greater the number of pixels each photo will contain. The more megapixels your image contains, the larger you can print it. My phone takes photos that I can print up to 48″ × 60″!

You need to know the numbers associated with your digital image to ensure the best-quality print for the sizes you want to use. People use the terms *dpi* and *ppi* interchangeably, adding to the confusion in terminology.

Add a Caption

Tuesday · Feb 15, 2022 · 1:29 PM   Adjust

IMG_0055

Apple iPhone XS Max   JPEG

Wide Camera — 26 mm ƒ1.8
8 MP · 2371 × 3190 · 1.7 MB

ISO 100   52mm   0 ev   ƒ1.8   1/66s

Photo size in pixels and photo information provided for each photo on newer devices

Resolutions of 72 Versus 300

Enlarged photo at 300 dpi resolution compared with original photo at 72 dpi resolution

The numbers 72 and 300 will pop up most frequently when you are working with digital photos and down-loaded images. A resolution of 72 dpi is the standard for online image viewing. If you enlarge an image that is a resolution of 72 dpi, you will see the pixels become more defined the larger you go.

A resolution of 300 is necessary for printing. When an image is set at a 300 dpi resolution, there is enough density in the image's pixels to provide a sharp print at any size.

Chances are that the photos taken on your phone and the ones you download from the internet will be saved at 72 dpi. Not to worry. The key is how many megapixels are in that 72-dpi image.

Image size and resolution do not go hand in hand. If you increase the print size of your photo but not the resolution, you may have a pixelated image. If you increase the resolution but not the number of pixels, the image will print smaller. For example,

a 42″ × 56″ image at 72 resolution has a print size of 7½″ × 10″ at 300 resolution.

Pixels-to-Inch Conversion

If you are able to view the size of your image in pixels on your device, you can find out what the existing printed image size will be.

Pixels divided by dpi = Inches

Fortunately, there are conversion charts available online that will calculate the print size based on the pixels per side. See the Resources section (page 127) for a user-friendly chart equating pixels to printable size.

Changing the Resolution

⮞ PERMISSION GRANTED ⮜

Before you use any apps you have downloaded to your device, go into your device settings and scroll down until you see the app name. Tap on the > and allow access to your photos. You may also have the option to select *All Photos* or *Selected Photos*. The apps won't work without this access.

Unless you have Adobe Photoshop or Adobe Lightroom, the best and easiest way to change the resolution of your photo to 300 dpi is with the paid Pro-level PicMonkey desktop app. There are a few other ways, but they are not as easy and straightforward.

How to Resize with PicMonkey

To *Resize > Smart Resize* scroll down to *Print Dimensions* and find your desired photo size. Click on *Resize*. Download (choose the *Print* option). Save to the desired folder. Voilá! You have just changed a small and low-res image into a large, ready-to-print, 300-dpi resolution image!

Resize with Image Size App for iOS and Android

This photo resizing app enables you to change an image to whatever size you like, quickly and easily. You can specify the output format using either pixels, millimeters, centimeters, or inches.

1. Open an image or take a photo

2. Crop the image by using your fingers to zoom in, if desired

3. Enter your desired output/print size in the *Width* and *Height* boxes

4. Choose options for the image: *Save/Share/Email/Print*

Easy Photo Size Change for Mac Computer

If you have a photo taken on a high-megapixel device or scanned at a 300 or higher-resolution, you can easily change the size of the photo on a Mac laptop or desktop computer. Click on the image file to open it in *Preview*, then choose *Select Tools*, then *Adjust Size*. A pop-up window opens with fields where you can change and enter a new image height, width, and resolution. Make sure both the *Scale Proportionally* and *Resample* boxes are checked to avoid distorting the resized image. Enter your desired print size and a resolution of 300 ppi. Save the file with a new name to keep both the original and the new image.

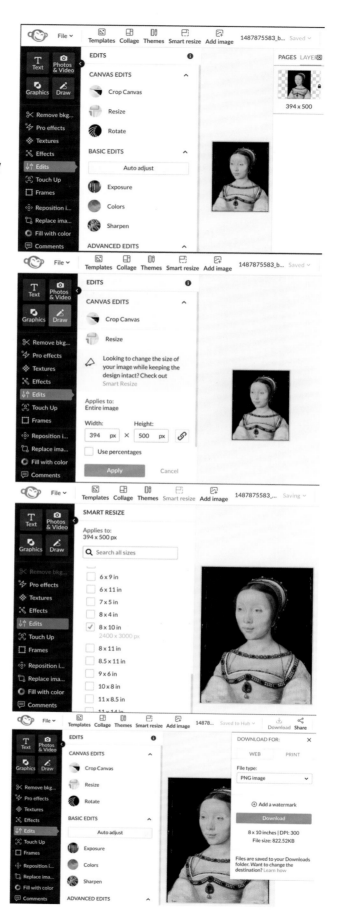

Got a Scanner?

If you have an old photo and a scanner, you also have the ability to create a higher resolution photo. Most scanners give you the option of choosing the resolution of the scanned image. If you want to enlarge the photo, scan and save it at 1,200 dpi—four times the resolution needed to produce a high-quality print! Scanning at 1,200 ppi increases the number of dots per inch of the photo, so when it is enlarged, there will be enough information to prevent pixelation.

After scanning and saving your image, open your image in *Preview* (Mac). Click on *Tools > Adjust Size*. Select *Inches* and enter the size you wish to print the image. It will automatically calculate the ratio based on the original size and may not equate to the exact dimensions you want. You can always crop it to fit in *Editing*. Change the resolution from 1,200 to 300 and click *OK*.

Photo Editing on Your Device

Photo editing home screen on an iPhone. The icons and photo editing actions are fairly standard across all types of devices.

Now that your photo is resized, the next step is to use the built-in photo editing apps on your phone or tablet to adjust the color, contrast, and brightness of your image and possibly crop it to highlight the desired focal point or detail. In most instances, you can turn a washed-out image into a beauty with just a few finger swipes.

≈ TIP ≈

If the photo you wish to edit is on your desktop, laptop, or other device, email or use AirDrop or Nearby Share to send it to your phone or tablet for easy editing.

The Power of the Crop

Before you dive into editing, I recommend that you determine whether a photo crop is in order. Cropping a photo can create more visual impact than all of your careful edits, repairs, or filters. The two major reasons to crop a photo are

- to remove unnecessary and distracting backgrounds
- to create a better composition.

A side benefit is that you will save time editing when there is less photo to work on.

Cropping enables your viewers to focus on the elements you want them to focus on. This draws them into the story of your memory quilt, creating drama. It is also an especially effective means to draw attention to a specific image if there is more than one on the quilt. Cropping a face can have a lot of impact. The larger the facial features, especially the eyes, the more the viewer can be drawn to the emotion within the face. This image enlargement and powerful crop of the photo is an excellent example of this in action.

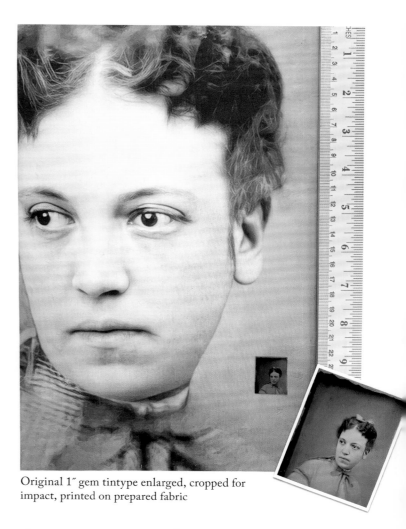

Original 1″ gem tintype enlarged, cropped for impact, printed on prepared fabric

⇒ CROPPING NOTES ⇐

- Crop your photos to tell a story.
- Leave out unnecessary details.
- Don't always center your subject.
- When cropping faces, leave some breathing room or quiet space.
- Crop above or below a body joint.

Because I wanted to see her smile and there's an app for that, I used FaceApp to put a smile on her face. Look at how it also changed the light in her eyes. Isn't artificial intelligence technology amazing?

Straighten First, Crop Second

Tap the *Crop* icon. If the angle of the photo appears crooked or skewed, choose one of the three *Crop Adjustment* tools and move the slider to straighten the photo or correct the vertical or horizontal perspective on the skewed image.

Drag the edges of the cropping box to crop the photo. You can also use your fingers to enlarge and zoom in on the image inside the cropping box before cropping. Look for additional symbols on the screen that will flip, rotate, or display typical preset crop proportions you can choose from.

Functions

Go to *Photos*, choose the photo, and tap *Edit* in the upper right corner. The image opens to an *Auto* editing option. Tap the wand to try it. This may be all you need to do to get the look you like. If not, tap the wand again to revert to the original. Begin to manually make the desired adjustments by swiping left to see all the available adjustment icons and their names.

ANDROID USERS! ↻ *Newer and updated phones have a hidden* Remaster *one-step artificial intelligence-based photo enhancement function that gives great results. Tap the three dots in the upper right corner and choose* Remaster *to auto-edit your image.*

Auto-edited image that I rejected

You can use the *Auto* editing function and slide control at the bottom of the screen to let the device do the work, but I find that it never looks as good as it should, especially when you are editing old photos. I use specific functions that will give me the look I want. Swipe the circles to reveal all the tools available for you to make precise adjustments. The functions I use most often are these:

- *Exposure* (to increase highlights if the photo is underexposed due to low light)

- *Brightness* (brightens the entire photo)

- *Black Point* (darkens the blacks for higher contrast)

- *Contrast* (increases the difference between light and dark areas, making light areas lighter and dark areas darker—a necessary action for faded old photos)

- *Saturation* or *Vibrance* (when needed)

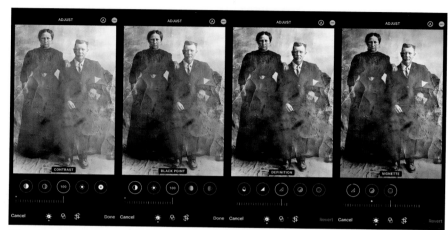

The editing functions I used in the order in which I applied them

Even if you are a pro, it is often worthwhile to see how *all* the functions look when applied to your photo. It is the best way to learn and hone your eye. The slider enables you to increase (or decrease) the intensity of the function's effect. You can see an example of that in the edits I made to the above photos where it was necessary to go to the full 100% for the *Contrast* and *Black Point* functions. That is definitely not always the case.

Filters

Tap the *Filters* icon to experiment with your device's built-in photo filters. These filters are used to give your photo different color temperatures and tone effects, such as *Vivid* or *Drama*. Or, try classic black-and-white looks like *Mono* and *Silvertone*.

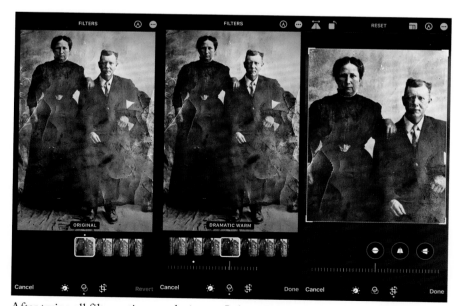

After trying all filter options on the image, I chose *Dramatic Warm* and decided to crop the photo to the focal point rather than trying to repair or restore the remainder of this old, damaged image.

Revert & Duplicate

Share icon

After you have saved an edited photo, you can always open it again in *Edit* and tap *Revert* to return it to the original, unedited image. Better yet, duplicate the new version first and then tap *Revert*, so you will have the original saved separately, in case you need it or wish to create a new version. The *Duplicate* option can be found by tapping the *Share* icon at the bottom left of the photo editing screen and scrolling down. The duplicated image will be saved to your photo library.

If you have updated your Apple device to iOS 16, (or higher), the *Duplicate* function is in a new location. After opening a photo, tap on the 3 dots in the circle at the upper right of the screen next to *Edit*. You'll find *Duplicate* and other functions on the new quick access dropdown menu.

Photo Repairs

The editing options built into your device are powerful, but they lack some necessary functionality. You may likely need to repair tears, scratches, age spots, stains, and other distracting marks or imperfections. This is when digital photo apps come to the rescue. There are many to choose from, and new ones pop up frequently. It is best to stick with one or two and get proficient, rather than try many. I use Snapseed, which is well-respected, free, and available for iOS and Android. It is used by professionals but is easy and intuitive enough for beginners. It includes advanced tools for professionals, simple editing tools for beginners, and plenty of effects and looks for all to play around with.

I primarily use Snapseed for its easy-to-use *Healing* adjustment tool and the more advanced *Curves* tool. With *Curves*, you can adjust brightness, contrast, highlights, and shadows all at the same time. Give it a try. Everything can be undone (look for the left-pointing arrow to revert.) It's digital, so nothing is ever wasted or ruined. The best way to learn how to use any tool is to play around with it to see what it does and how you can use it to further your vision.

INSIDE APP SETTINGS *Before using any app, go to the app's* Settings. *If the option is present, set the size of the photo output to the highest available, since you will be printing the app version of the photo.*

How to Use the Snapseed *Healing* Tool

Screenshots of the Snapseed *Healing* tool from tool selection to final image export

The *Healing* tool is a necessary photo repair tool that enables you to erase or blend areas that need a touch-up, such as scratches, cracks, or age spots on vintage photos. You can also remove distracting objects, such as power lines, or other people from the photo.

1. Import your photo into Snapseed.

2. Tap on Tools and select Healing. You will see your image on the screen.

3. Spread 2 fingers open to enlarge the image, move it around, and zoom in to the section you need to repair or heal. (You will see a box in the lower left that indicates the visible portion of the workspace in the overall photo.) Remove your fingers from the screen.

4. Use your index or smaller pinky finger to tap or brush over on the spot that you wish to heal. You will see a red area signifying where your changes will be made. That area will be replaced with pixels from the surrounding area. The Healing tool in Snapseed does not allow you to choose the exact location of the pixels being used to replace (heal) the image, so you may see that it borrows the wrong pixels from the adjacent area. Simply use the reverse arrow at the bottom to redo. Often, zooming in closer will help. It may take a little bit of practice to get the feel for it, but once you do, you will discover how valuable a tool it is.

5. When you are happy with your image, tap on the checkmark to save the image. You will return to the main screen. To save the image, tap on Export, which will save the photo as a new image in your photo library.

≈ USE A STYLUS ≈

A digital stylus that pairs with your device can be used instead of a finger for precision tasks like using the *Healing* tool. I use an Apple pencil.

Ultimately, the original photograph was too damaged for me to complete all of the desired edits on my device. I used Photoshop on my desktop so I would have more options and greater control over the outcome.

Photo Manipulation—When & Why

Manipulate: *v.* to change by artful means so as to serve one's purpose

There's a difference between editing a photo and manipulating it to be something *more or other than* the original photo. The act of editing and repairing maintains and improves the original photograph. Manipulating a photograph adds (or subtracts) appearance and details that did not exist in the original. As an artist creating in the digital age, I use originals to create new art by manipulating photos digitally, using a variety of easily accessible free or inexpensive apps. Surprisingly, "photographers from the get-go were working hard to alter images" (Clive Thomas, "Pictures That Deceive," *Smithsonian*, December 2021). From the beginning

A circus-life effect on this fun, over-the-top manipulated photograph

days of photography in 1839, they were manipulating photos in the darkroom and considering this to be a new artistic technique. They found it to be as exciting as I do.

There are apps that use preset filters, called Looks or Overlays, to create a variety of effects, such as tintype, vintage, cyanotype, watercolor, sketch, paint, recolor, pop art, cartoon, mosaic, imitative rendering of famous artists' styles, gothic, add text, rubber stamp, posterize, bokeh (the way a lens renders out-of-focus points of light), backgrounds, and more. Many photo-altering apps are geared toward social media posts, gimmicks, and other such purposes, but there are some very useful and effective ones that are used by artists and professional photographers. I use a select few on a regular basis, chosen for their ease of use, their cost (usually free), and the quality and presentation of the functions they offer.

Modern digital photo made to look like a tintype using a tintype app

Invaluable Apps

There are two very helpful apps I recommend if you are working with old photographs. They use amazing artificial intelligence (AI) algorithms to automatically sharpen facial features and colorize black-and-white photos. The results aren't always spot-on, but the outcomes are usually much better than what you start with.

- Remini is an AI app that will turn a blurred photo into a sharper image. It is particularly useful for facial features. If you have a grainy, damaged, or low-resolution photo, it will render a clear, sharp, high-definition image.

- Colorize is an AI app that does just that. The software can recognize different objects and determine their likely colors. It will read a black-and-white image and produce a color image—not the actual colors, mind you, but the inexplicable AI colors determined by subject matter. It will turn a lawn green and a dress blue, and render a realistic complexion and eye color.

Before and after photos using Remini app for photo adjustment

COLONEL NINIA ℓ BEALL

My ancestor, colorized. Interestingly, the eyes were rendered as the same color blue as my father's!

Artful Apps

It's easy to get carried away with all the filters and options available today. I create a lot of photos just for fun and practice, but when it comes to creating a manipulated photo for a finished project, I ask myself, does the apps' output

- add to or advance the story?

- create a desired mood or suggestion of time?

- positively jar expectations?

- intentionally draw attention to strengthen the composition?

- unintentionally draw too much attention?

- challenge the viewer to see with new eyes?

- add to or detract from the overall visual composition and quilt top?

Tempering App Fever

Certain images create private little excitements in the brain.
— E. L. DOCTOROW —

I can fall in love with an idea or a look and become blinded to the big picture, so here is a trick I use to knock me back to my artistic senses. I take a photograph of the work-in-progress and see if my attention gets stuck on the manipulated photo. It will often show up as an outpoint when seen through a new lens. If you still want to use a specific manipulated photo, look for ways to make it play well with the other parts of the composition. Case in point: I subdued the color of the Anna Atkins photo in *Cyano Anna* (page 68) so it would blend in better and not be the first thing people would see. I also played around with the size to reduce the impact.

(L–R) Original black-and-white photo of Anna Atkins; colorized version, two-step SketchMee and PaintMee2 version, and the final subdued-color version

Photo Printing

A sampling of photo alterations and effects on a variety of surfaces.

(L-R from top)

Row 1: Colorized image printed on prepared fabric; blurred image TAP transfer on bleached muslin; original image TAP transfer on muslin

Row 2: Original image on-demand printed on chiffon; BeCasso colorized and altered image TAP transfer on bleached muslin; original image TAP transfer on hand-dyed cotton)

Row 3: Stamp-effect image on pieced quilt fragment; original image on-demand printed on cotton; stamp-effect TAP transfer on Essex linen

Row 4: Sketch-effect TAP transfer on bleached muslin; cyanotype print on prepared fabric; direct print on Lutradur, rough-coated with gesso and inkAID

(Public domain photo of Helen L. Gilson, Civil War nurse)

You have completed the necessary digital editing and manipulation of your photo. Now it's time to bring it off the screen and onto the fabric. This step in the memory quilt process is also full of options and choices.

Printer Settings

Paper (fabric) size

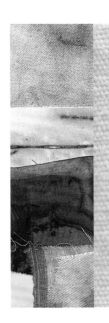

You have the option of printing at several preset sizes. You just have to decide on the setting before you print. Options include letter or legal size, borderless or not. If Custom settings are available, you can enter the dimensions of your paper-bakced fabric sheet; for instance, if the fabric is cut to 5″ × 7″ and you are printing a 4″ × 6″ image, you will not waste any of your prepared fabric.

All printers are different, but generally, print your images at a plain paper setting unless otherwise instructed by the substrate manufacturer.

☙ MAKING FABRIC PRINTER READY ☙

Iron your fabric to freezer paper, fuse onto Lutradur, or apply a spray-on or soak-in fabric stiffener (I use Terial Magic). Trim the tips of the two corners that feed into the printer at a 45° angle to prevent the paper-backed fabric from jamming.

Pre-printing Checklist

1. Make sure your device or computer screen is at, or close to, full illumination so you can accurately assess colors.

2. Check your ink levels before printing. When a color is low and just before you get the message to change it, it can (in my experience) cause a shift in the other colors it mixes with or, in the case of black ink, cause streaking.

3. Always arrive at the final size of the photo by printing it in only black ink on paper. It is cheaper to print on paper while fine-tuning the size for use in your quilt. I will often print two sizes (if they fit horizontally on one sheet) so I can compare, for example, a 4″ × 6″ and a 5″ × 7″ photo, to see which one works best in the composition.

Remember, size is an art element and faces are always a focal point, so the size of the photo plays an important part in the overall composition.

4. Print your image in color on paper before printing on your final surface. The color and brightness you see on your screen don't always translate to paper, and even less so when printed onto fabric. I do a page of small test swatches of my photos on the final surface before the final printing by reducing the image size and grouping several onto one page. Test swatches save me heartache and ink.

5. Once the final edits are complete, I always lighten the image before printing it onto fabric or TAP. What looks too light on my computer screen usually prints just right on those surfaces.

☙ NOTHING WASTED ☙

Recycle, reuse, recolor, and in other ways conserve your test prints in your journal, in a collage, as a project record, or as a base for sketching or gelli printing. My motto is that nothing art-related is ever trash.

Printing Surfaces

It should come as no surprise that I am partial to TAP Transfer Artist Paper for transferring photos onto fabric. But as you can see, it is not the only method I use. My goals for each memory quilt dictate what I choose to print the image on, which, in turn, helps me better convey the story I am telling. You can see excellent examples of a variety of methods and the resulting photos on fabric in the eight projects (see Projects, pages 64–89) and the work of 21 contributing artists shown throughout this book and in the Gallery (pages 90–125).

You may already have experience in one or more of these methods. (I use them all.) I surveyed a group of quilters who print photos onto fabric. Based on their comments and my experience, there are pros and cons of each method and reasons why you might or might not want to use each one. Remember, no matter how or where you print your image on fabric, the best results will come from the effort you put into making your photos print-worthy.

NOTE ℗ *I have not evaluated the washability or durability of these surfaces since memory quilts are considered art, which is not subject to washing.*

Direct Printing on Fabric

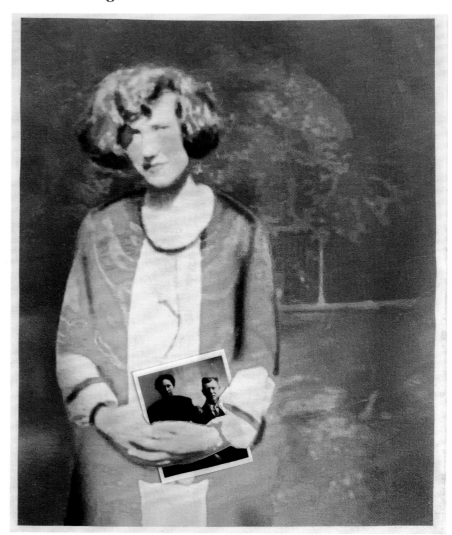

Large photo of my great-aunt, Alease, printed on fabric and then cut at the hands to insert the tiny, edited TAP transfer photo of her parents

I have been printing directly on fabric since the first home color printers became available, first on fabric that I pre-treated with Bubble Jet Set, then on commercially pretreated, paper-backed fabric. I still use pre-treated fabric occasionally. The different brands of prepared fabric vary in quality, thread count, whiteness, and type of fabric available, with cotton being the most common.

⇒ CUT YOUR OWN ⇐

Buy a roll of prepared fabric and cut pieces to size as needed. While the initial outlay may be high, it is more cost-effective in the long run and gives you more size options than the packaged sheets. Share the cost with friends or consider a guild purchase.

- Quick and easy

- Easy to sew

- Maintains the fabric hand

- Commercially available

CONS

- Pigment printer ink (versus water-based ink) is recommended even for pretreated fabric to prevent future fading

- Need to back with freezer paper, fuse to Lutradur, or use spray stiffener for printing

- Prepared fabric is costly

- Can dull the image

- Not UV resistant

- May take several attempts at color adjustments to get the image to your liking

On-Demand Digital Printing

We live in an era when we finally have access to having our photos, art, or designs commercially printed on fabric as small runs. Not only that, but there is also a range of fabrics to print on, and you can group as many photos as you want on a fat quarter or a yard. I use the service when I want to print an image larger than my wide-carriage printer can accommodate. You should always order a test swatch first to check the color.

PROS

- Can group several images on a yard or fat quarter

- Can print larger images than with your home printer

- Conserves your printer ink

- Don't need a supply of print-ready fabric

CONS

- Recommended test swatch increases the wait for the final product

- Can take up to two weeks or more to receive

- Can be expensive

- Not resistant to ultraviolet light

- Some will not withstand dyeing

- Learning curve for uploading and placement of your digital images

My vision for the quilt was grand, so I enlarged this tiny photo and sent it off to be printed on-demand. (I used Spoonflower.)

TAP Transfer Artist Paper

I introduced TAP Transfer Artist Paper to the market in 2010 as a welcome alternative to the acrylic-medium transfers I had been using for several years. It is an easy-to-source, and simple-to-use iron-on transfer paper that provides sharp, color-saturated, fade-proof images. The polymer coating on the paper encloses both water-based and pigment inks, and seals them *into* the fabric. You can find complete information and instructions in my recent book, *The Ultimate Guide to Transfer Artist Paper* (C&T Publishing).

PROS

- Transfers will not fade or abrade

- Can group several images on a sheet

- Ability to tile, print, and transfer large images

- Can use water-based or pigment printer inks

- Easy to sew

- Can be used on a variety of fabrics and surfaces

- Trimmed edges of transfers do not fray

- Easily takes to hand coloring and painting both before and after transferring

- Advice and troubleshooting available from the creator (that's me!)

CONS

- Changes the hand of the fabric (the lower the thread count, the softer the hand)

- Uses printer inks

- Best used on white or light fabrics

- Can be expensive

- Must print images in reverse for transfers

- Inkjet printer only

TAP transfers on copper mesh,
gold leather, and cotton organdy

Cyanotype

Cyanotype is a cameraless photographic printing method discovered in 1842. Two chemicals, when mixed together, become light-sensitive and develop when exposed to sunlight. Any objects placed on the fabric that block out the sun will result in a white print. You can purchase prepared fabric or prepare your own. To transfer a photo, you create a film negative of the image. The major cyanotype solution supplier has an easy-to-use negative generator on its website, along with complete instructions (See Resources, page 127).

PROS

- Free sun exposure method
- Does not use up color ink
- Easy and safe for children
- Comparatively inexpensive
- Can print on a variety of natural fiber surfaces

CONS

- Need sunshine or a professional lighting setup
- Results will always be blue
- Requires a film negative
- Best if used on white or light fabric

A variety of cyanotype prints on fabric.
The portrait was created with a film negative.

Two negatives were printed and layered together to provide the best contrast for cyanotype printing.

SolarFast

Similar to cyanotype, SolarFast is a recent cameraless photographic printing method developed by Jacquard Products owner Asher Katz in 2013. Unlike the cyanotype process, it has several color options. It also requires the sun and a film negative for photo printing.

Solarfast print on cotton

PROS

- 14 mixable colors
- Permanent dye
- Easy to sew

CONS

- Must be applied and exposed while wet
- More of a learning curve than cyanotype
- Exposure times can vary
- Has a limited shelf life

InkAID

A digital ground pre-coat for inkjet printers, inkAID enables printing on a variety of surfaces and substrates that usually don't take kindly to printers. Creator Jim Kedenburg introduced the product in 2013 and is always available for assistance and advice. It really can open up a world of printing possibilities. For more information and in-depth instructions, see Wen Redmond's *Digital Fiber Art: Combine Photos & Fabric: Create Your Own Mixed-Media Masterpiece* (C&T Publishing).

PROS

- Can print on a variety of surfaces such as Lutradur, aluminum foil, canvas, rough surfaces, painted surfaces, and more

CONS

- One-year shelf life
- Inkjet printer only
- Must prepare surface with solution before printing
- Needs time to dry
- May be expensive

Other Methods

Two of the contributing artists used methods outside of the scope of this book to print their images onto fabric. Suzanne Coley (page 112) is a master at hand-cut linoleum block printing. Taking her inspiration from a photo or her imagination, she can carve emotion into a block like no other. Award-winning art quilter Patty Kennedy-Zafred (page 122) silkscreens selected public domain photographs onto her own hand-dyed shibori fabrics, honoring and enriching the history she loves to print.

Perhaps you have a skill or a method that has not been covered in this book or other transfer methods like Thermofax printing, intaglio, or machine sketching. How can you use your technique knowledge and skills to create a memorable image on fabric?

⇒ FRAYING FIX ⇐

Back your photos with fusible web before trimming. (I use Mistyfuse.)

he angel doesn't sit on your shoulder unless the p
dventure or nothing. Helen Keller We are all visionari
miel The human race does command its own destin
tars. Lorraine Hansberry How old would you be if you di
ope of life by untying its knots. Jean Toomer This is th
isorder of life that order which is art. James Baldwin V
hreshold of a new dawn. Martin Luther Ling, Jr. What do
ou leave behind? Sandra Sharp My impressions are sc
nemory. Etty Hillesum We are not here to see through
amott Within you there is stillness and a sanctuary
ermann Hesse Each thing she learned became part of
ate Seredy Music is well said to be the speech of ange
ohn O'Donohue The face is the mirror of the mind and
eart. St. Jerome An image is a bridge between evoked
One cannot divine nor forecast the conditions that
hem by chance, in a lucky hour. Willa Cather It is in o
ruth sometimes comes to the top. Virginia Woolf To ex
ife of emotions is to make art. Jane Heap The real mo
rowd. George Bernard Shaw When you learn to love and
earth of your own spirit. You are completely at o
ohn O'Donohue Nobody knows what I am trying to do
ike any art, the creation of self is both natural and
s magic. Holly Near The personal, if it is deep enough
nais Nin It began in mystery, and it will end in myste

Print on canvas, assisted by inkAID

Narrative Quilting

Narratives are the threads that bind us.
— MARK NEPO —

Ten of Cups, 30″ × 40′″

My mother's collection of silver baby cups that held one memory for her, another for me

Narrative quilts, also known as story quilts, have a long history. They act as historical documents that preserve narratives about place and identity. Quilts are a narrative part of many cultures. People of different times, countries, and cultures have used cloth-based art forms to pass down their traditions and oral history. A quilt's surface can often be "read" through symbols and graphic cues. From the choice of material to the design and patterns, these quilts can tell stories about the time period in which they were made and the people who made them.

Perhaps the first, definitely the best-known, narrative quilts were created by Harriet Powers. Born in 1837 as a slave, she could neither read nor write. In the late 1800s, she created two dramatic and powerful story quilts that continue to have a major impact on women and quilting.

Bible Quilt, 1886, by Harriet Powers (public domain)

A friendship quilt made and gifted by my students is now a memory of a wonderful workshop on Whidbey Island.

"The narrative quilt tells a story, preserves a history, or celebrates a societal milestone. Some of these quilts celebrate progress (women's suffrage centennial quilts), some preserve a painful history so that it isn't forgotten (forced migration quilts), still others explore identity and heritage. They say history is written by the victors, but quilters from diverse backgrounds have used quilting to record and preserve their own experiences for subsequent generations. The quilts … pass on stories, feelings and perspectives that have defined the quilter's life in some way and are meant to inspire generations to come." ("Activist Quilts: An Introduction," Simmons College Library, simmonslis.libguides.com/activistquilts)

Telling Your Story

Your family history, dreams, memories, and stories are often built on fragments and slender threads of evidence. Don't let a lack of information stop you. Begin with what you have available to you and then take poetic license to fill in the rest of the story. Add details or use fabrics that convey memories such as "She always wore a red ribbon in her hair," "She had a love of stripes," or "She had a dog named Blue." Consider using actual objects—glasses, charms, letters, lockets, tickets, ephemera. To visually enrich the story, add relatable references and contribute details that reinforce your story.

Details help tell the story shared in Anne Sonner's memory quilt (page 118).

There is a strong relationship between stories and quilts. A quilt can represent a personal story or one inspired by a person, special occasion, or place. Quilts are made to tell both personal and shared history. During the Civil War, women sewed quilts for soldiers. Sometimes they'd write messages or poems in ink onto the quilt itself before sending it to the front. One Sunday school teacher printed her mailing address on her quilt so wounded soldiers could start a correspondence with her. What messages, hidden or visible, might you add to your quilt?

Think of a narrative quilt as a way to visually paraphrase your memory. Take the gist of the story and use fabrics, colors, and imagery to create a feeling or contribute a sense of place and time. First and foremost, let your emotions guide you. Use what matters to you. To honor means to keep what is true *in view*, not to depict it exactly. Create with ideas and materi-

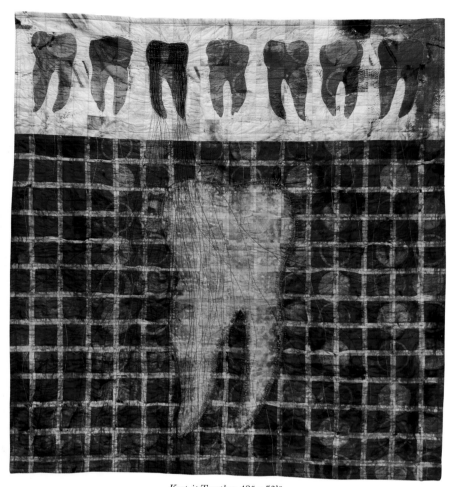

Keep it Together, 48˝ × 53′˝

Kim Eichler-Messmer's memory quilt is personal, yet the story is not clear, allowing room for us to bring our own interpretation to the quilt.

als that relate to the story, but allow the story to develop spontaneously as you build the quilt. It probably will, anyway, so don't fight it. Be flexible in response to what comes and trust your intuition. It's okay to abandon your original plan in midstream.

Be memory driven, not technique driven. Quilt police cannot dictate your self-expression or your memory. In the end, it is the story that will resonate with people, not the construction details. Bring the memory into focus. Aim for authenticity over perfection.

My tendency (which I am forever trying to overcome) is to represent things too literally, wanting viewers to know exactly what they are looking at and to understand what I am saying. That, of course, is not always necessary and may or may not be your way of working. Keep in mind that some stories are about feelings and impressions rather than specific moments or events. Clarity is not a virtue, especially for art. Go with your gut.

Photo Quilt Design

The most personal is the most creative.
— MARTIN SCORSESE —

When creating your memory quilt, you are in full control of what you make others see and feel. That can be both exciting and scary. Making your quilt is not complicated when you think of it as working in layers—layers of meaning, fabric, photo, stitch, and story. Everything should work together to convey your memory.

We've all seen a quilt or work of art that is technically perfect but leaves us cold. We have also been drawn to a quilt that has obvious flaws or is less than "perfect." Why does one quilt move you and another not? Art created by untrained outsider artists, naïve artists, and children all have one thing in common: these creators completely put themselves into their art. There is no holding back. There is no critical self-evaluation.

Composition and technical skills should always be secondary to *you*. You are the most important element of your art. You must be willing to create less-than-perfect work in order to create art that resonates with others. Perfection is the enemy. You, your story, your vision—you are the hero.

So how do you avoid perfectionism and still create a wonderful quilt? What if I told you that you could avoid all that anguish associated with creating, by making the "right" design decisions? What if you could just bypass all the doubt and second-guessing? What if I told you that the reassurance you are looking for is right under your nose?

This thing, this confidence that you are looking for, is something so obvious that it is often easily overlooked or dismissed as too simple to be meaningful. It is something that you have had with you all along but rarely take the time to get to know.

"What is right under my nose?" you ask. Go on. See for yourself. Look down. Your answer is there, right under your nose.

That thing you insist on looking for outside of yourself is hidden within your heart.

I don't think it's a coincidence that *art* is a part of *heart*. Work from your heart, not your head.

Things gathered that catch my eye. My design board offers clues to my style.

Your style comes from your heart. Style is the imprint of your personality on your art. It's the *you* in your quilt. If you allow yourself to work from your heart, your own style will emerge. Your work will be as unique as you are; it can't help but be because nobody has seen the world through your eyes, lived your experiences, felt your emotions, or gathered your stories.

Your style can be imparted with:

- Color
- Materials
- Pattern
- Narrative
- Signature techniques
- Subject matter
- Repeated elements
- And so much more

⟫ DESIGN BOARD, BOX, OR BOOK ⟪

If you want to discover your style, start gathering images, fabric bits and pieces, and anything else that deserves a second look or inspires you. Pin them, glue them in a journal, or drop in a box. Revisit and review them often. You will begin to notice the repeating art elements and principles that are echoed in your heart. Use this information and awareness to guide your quilt design.

Delight-full Writing/Sketching Exercise

Grab a notebook or journal and something to write with. You may want to include some colored pencils or fabric swatches and glue.

- Define your style
- Describe the ways you impart your style
- Dig deeper
- Declare your memory quilt intentions
- Discover story artifacts (letters, maps, photos)
- Develop the quilt plan

- Determine what you'll need (fabrics, photos for printing, mementos, batting, etc.)
- Do the work

Photos, Fabric & Composition

Arrange whatever pieces come your way.
— VIRGINIA WOOLF —

Composition is the necessary bones or framework that you use to build your memory quilt on. It serves to support your materials, your emotion, your story, and your memory. It is the putting together of parts or elements to form a whole.

I'm not good at sewing but I know how to put things together so that you can see what I see.
— PENNY SISTO, QUILTER —

Composition is a range, not a finite target. It goes from bad—glaring outpoints that everyone notices, to good—subtle nuances that only the trained eye can detect, to great—in work that sings! You are automatically creating a composition (good, bad, or in-between) every time you create art.

Range of composition

> ### ☙ GO EASY ON YOURSELF ☙
>
> There is no perfect composition, so let me tell you this right now; do not aim for perfection. You will never make it. Go for good. Go for better. Go for your best. But don't try to be perfect. Perfect is an endlessly moving target. It always has been and always will be out of reach. Do not get caught up in perfection paralysis. There will always be another quilt to make.

Composition is a means to create better art. Understanding composition helps you solve problems you encounter when you are creating art. Understanding composition makes you a better artist. It holds the answer when you feel that something is just not right.

Composition is a result and a by-product of quiltmaking. Composition happens whether you pay attention to it or not. Just as some people have a natural talent for drawing, others may have a natural talent for composition. They do it intuitively. The opposite is also true. Some people may be composition-blind (similar to tone-deaf) and just don't see when an artwork is somehow "off." Most of us fall somewhere between.

Like Goldilocks, we want to create a composition with shapes, colors, textures and other elements that are not too dull, not too distressing, but "just right."
— GREG ALBERT —

The Elements of Composition

- Line
- Shape/Form
- Value/Light
- Texture
- Space/Size
- Movement/Time
- Color

Detail of *From the Neighborhood*

Notice how the frayed threads contribute to and enhance the stitched lines and create movement, working together with the faded photo to suggest time.

Art elements are a *result* of creating art. Draw and you create line. Collage creates shapes. Paint, stitch, or glue things on a canvas or quilt, and you are creating space. The elements are the tools you use when you create your art.

They are the frame of reference you refer to when you are trying to improve what you are creating, if you have indecision about the placement of color or direction of movement, you consult what you know about these elements and how they relate to art principles.

The Principles of Composition

- Contrast
- Dominance/Focal Point
- Balance
- Proportion/Scale
- Repetition/Pattern/Rhythm
- Variety
- Harmony/Unity

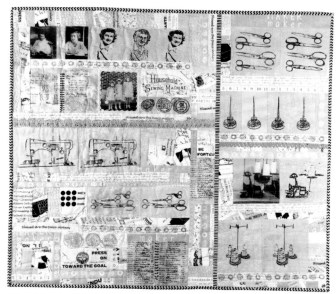

Blessed Are the Piecemakers, 35″ × 32″ by Susan L. Price
Which design principles were used in this memory quilt?

Principles are the rules that you apply to the elements. Art principles are the visual components that give structure to expression. One of the most important of these is contrast. *Contrast* refers to the arrangement of opposite elements and effects, for example, light and dark colors, smooth and rough textures, and large and small shapes. Contrast can be used to create variety, visual interest, and drama in an artwork.

The scale of this quilt top assists the story by magnifying the magical experience I had being this close to the deer.

Let's Face It

As humans, it is our nature and instinct to look at a face first. A face on a quilt will always be the focal point unless you take strong measures to lessen its impact. Size/scale and color are two art elements you can use to reduce the impact, as I did with the portrait in my quilt in homage to Anna Atkins, *Cyano Anna* (page 68).

Follow the eyes. When using photos of people or portraits, place them so that the eyes look inward on the quilt, not out, off the edge. (Unless looking outward is part of the story!) This keeps the viewer´s eyes on your quilt. Mirror-image the photo if necessary.

How do the size and positioning of the faces and direction of the gazes lead the eye through this fabric collage?

In art, as in nature, we tend to prefer balance. It is comforting and reassuring. Good composition keeps the viewer's eye moving through the piece, not just locked on your focal point. This is helped by contrasting light and dark areas, small and large shapes, positive and negative spaces, quiet areas and busy areas. Create contrast and interest by juxtaposing textured and flat areas, large and small prints, contrasting colors, straight lines and curved. Remember to leave space to breathe, a rest for the eye.

➤ EXPOSING CONTRAST ➤

Take a black-and-white photo to check the contrast of the fabric and elements on your quilt top.

Notice the contrasting combination in the repetition and variety Whitney Dahlberg created in her quilt, *Reflections* (page 114). Observe how the color story enhances the celebratory memory story in Susan Brubaker Knapp's quilt, *The Graduate* (page 116). See how Katherine Stewart Wilson uses repetition of shapes and sizes to pull the eye around and create movement in her quilt, *Grandma's Hands* (page 92).

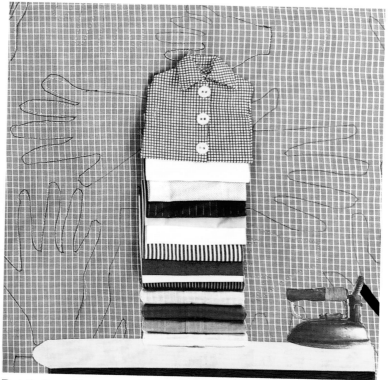

Detail of repetition in *Grandma's Hands* (page 92) by Katherine Stewart Wilson

Composition Exercise

Download and use this Composition Checklist to help you understand the workings of the elements and principles. See them in action by looking at all the quilts in this book. With your Checklist in hand, make note of how the artists use specific art elements and principles in their composition, and how these, in turn, create a significant contribution to the story or memory. Print more copies to use when you are creating your quilt.

Composition Checklist

ELEMENTS	PRINCIPLES						
	Dominance	Balance	Proportion/ Scale	Repetition	Rhythm	Variety	Harmony/ Unity
Line							
Shape/Form							
Value/Light							
Texture							
Space							
Movement/ Time							
Color							

Download a Composition Checklist

My composition checklist can be accessed through a tiny URL. To access the checklist just type the tiny URL (a web address) into your browser window. When you type your tiny URL into your browser window, the digital file will open up, and you can download and print the chart.

tinyurl.com/11483-patterns-download

Everything that becomes a part of the quilt rectangle, or shape, must relate in some way to everything else that is already there. Some attributes, however subtle or slight, must be shared between some or all of the other elements. Don't get hung up on this. If you follow along with what I have been saying, it should happen intuitively. When you are finished with the design process, if something just isn't right, use your knowledge of compositional elements and principles to weed out or remedy the offender.

Got Feelings?

I have a morning practice of devouring art books, fashion and home decor magazines, and Instagram posts. I am on a constant lookout to fill my bottomless well of inspiration, even while walking in nature or driving through country roads or city streets. My morning practice of a daily dose of inspiration makes it easier for me to connect ideas, colors, and techniques into a vision, especially when I'm not focused on the quilt or artwork at hand. I think of it as a way to keep my design eye sharp. If I see something that draws my attention, I'll stop, ask myself why, and then seek out the way compositional elements and principles were used to make me stop and look.

What mood do these hand-dyed and rusted fabrics create? What else do you notice about them?

A photo memory quilt will always express a mood or emotion and engage the viewer's feelings, intentionally or not, so why not make it intentional? My daily practice provides me with many examples of this. Studying these found images, rather than just flipping through the pages or swiping up, really hones the eye and sensibility (plus it's fun and a way to justify looking at art versus creating art). You can elicit emotion, control or change mood, or try on other moods just by changing the fabrics you choose, the colors you use, and their values, implied age, or excitement level. All of the elements and principles of art are creative tools that come into play when you are telling a story. Consider how these options might make you feel:

- A tiny photo on a large, vast solid-color space

- A tightly cropped face on a busy abstract print with diagonals and high contrast

- A pale, desaturated color image on a rusted vintage fabric

A quilt's mood can also be created with the use of textual, spatial, and graphic clues. For example, will your family photos be close together or spread apart? Is one larger than the others? Are the color choices cheery or somber? The image is not the only part of the quilt that will be telling the story.

Creating Your Visual Memories

With making comes meaning.
— CAS HOLMES—

My memory quilts always start with a photo. There will be something about the photo or the story it suggests that makes me want to know more, to research, recall, or imagine the story behind it. After the image and its story, color and pattern play drive my design choices, especially as to how they will relate to and enhance the story. I start with a sense of where I am going, initially led by the story and photo, and allow the fabrics, images, and composition to help lead the way.

Let the memory guide you. You don't need it all worked out before you begin, just follow your instinct and heart. Focus on what has meaning for you. The answers will come in the doing. Great work often comes from play. If it feels right but seems a little (or a lot) wacky, run with it and see where it leads you. Live with it a while if you have to.

The construction of your quilt is a linear process, but the design process is circuitous and continuous. It is not complete until you take the last stitch. Making a memory quilt, a memory *art* quilt, is a multifaceted process. Creating is always a breeding ground for new ideas and unlimited possibilities. In fact, the creative process really revs up while you are *at work* on your initial idea. Make room for

things to happen during the process. Your original plan might change, and that's likely a good thing!

My Mother Before Me, 38˝ × 48˝

Separate stories joined together as a whole

That said, beware of trying to fit too much onto one quilt. Rather than try to tell a whole life story, narrow down a concept, highlight, or specific memory. Pull those highlights or focal points from the person, place, or thing, and then choose what it is you really want to say. If you try to share too much or too many pieces of the story, it's like trying to read a run-on sentence. Creating a larger quilt so you can add more information isn't always a solution. The larger you work, the harder it is to nail down a good composition. That takes practice. Instead, create a small series of quilts. These can be displayed separately or joined together as separate pieces of a greater whole, as seen in *My Mother Before Me*.

Choosing Fabrics

Fabric, material, textile, cloth, fiber: Fabric has many names and uses in our lives. It is a form of self-expression and holds meaning for us, from birth to death. It is also an art medium. More importantly, it is an art *element*, one that consists of many art elements and principles. This is why your fabric choices are such an important, powerful, and integral part of designing your quilt.

Designing your memory quilt starts with your photo in hand and a visit to your fabric stash. But don't start that irresistibly fun part of the process just yet. Read on so you know what to look for.

A small selection from my large stash

I want to promote the consciousness of cloth. Textiles are an extension of our bodies and an essential part of human life—they connect us to our past, and to each other.
— JORDANA MUNK MARTIN —

Certain fabrics have deep connotations and evoke memory. Some may be universal, but most are specific to time, place, race, culture, and story. For me, they are schoolgirl plaids, vintage kitchen dish towels, antique lace collars, crisp white linen, seersucker, madras, and the slubby appeal of iridescent dupioni silk. While I choose my fabrics at random, I always try to (re)create a mood or a memory, or evoke a time or a place. Keep this in mind when you work. Does the fabric remind you of Victorian parlor wallpaper, a spring garden, or a summer beach? What image would complement the fabric? What fabric would enhance the message in the image you have chosen?

It still amazes me that an image can be interpreted in so many different ways just through the fabrics you choose and use, or the words in a quote you include. A young girl's face can look dreamy or determined depending on the message in the quote. A background of schoolgirl plaid can reinforce that message of determination, while rich brocade will set you to dreaming along with the woman in the photo.

> **≈ TIP ≈**
>
> Unusual color combinations can draw attention to a subject or area, delight, create vibrancy, and make the quilt sing.

Unexpected facial colors and fabric choices draw you in and hold your interest. What story might each of these be hinting at or telling?

I don't think I have to convince you that a large fabric stash is helpful, a necessity perhaps. When making an art memory quilt it is important to me to have a variety of fabric types: cotton, linen, silk in all its glorious weaves, brocades, jacquards, velvets, and sheers, to name a few. You'll want a variety of patterns and scales, both large and small, to create contrast and interest. Texture tantalizes. And color—one can never have enough color. To

paraphrase UK painter, printmaker, and collage artist Mark Hearld, quilters "need a lot of colors just like writers need a lot of words. … Ultimately what matters is how they're combined." More than anything, I love combining fabric, much as a poet combines words. It is my way of communicating emotion and story.

Choose colors, patterns, textures, and prints that augment the story you are creating. That does not mean that you always need to choose the obvious fabrics. For example, a Civil War story quilt does not need to be made with reproduction Civil War fabrics, *unless* they are integral to the story you are telling in that particular quilt. The fabrics I selected for the quilt I made to celebrate my great-grandmother's wedding-day photograph are totally unexpected, given the era of the photograph. I wanted to give her portrait a modern interpretation and contrast it with fabrics you might have seen the year I got married. What element do you see repeated in this quilt, and why do you think I chose the colors I did?

Matilda's Wedding Day, 24″ × 24″

> **≈ DIY FABRICS ≈**
>
> Don't see what you need, or have a certain vision in mind? Consider dyeing, overdyeing, painting, overpainting, stamping, mark-making, or printing your own. Add surface design with what's on hand.

Fabric Checkpoint

Before you cut into your fabric, answer these ten questions. There are no wrong answers. The intention is to listen to your heart and learn how to hone your eye. It may also be helpful to do the exercise on the four samples shown in Choosing Fabrics (page 50).

• Upon first look, what element (fabric) dominates?

• Which fabrics create texture?

• What two fabrics provide the most contrast and why?

• What elements and principles are present in your fabric color selections?

• Which fabric(s) imply or visually create movement?

• Take note of the proportion and size of each piece of fabric that you've laid out. What do you notice?

• What is your favorite fabric and why?

• Does this favorite fabric relate to a memory? How can you build on this memory with other fabrics?

• Which fabric do you like the least, and why?

• How does this least-liked fabric relate to the overall composition? What purpose might it serve?

Collage Quilting

Fun and exploration are not an inherent part of the creative process, they are necessary.
– ARMANDO MESÍAS –

My collage style of quilting was born out of necessity. With an overflow of burning desire to create but at a loss for space, I was forced to work flat on the only clear space I could find, my bed. I had to clear it off every night, but it was a set-up that served me well for several years. Looking back, I now realize that I have been in love with and committed to the art and process of putting gathered things together to tell a story. The art of collage relies heavily on composition and, like piecing a quilt, it combines many pieces to make a wondrous whole.

Read & Reflect, 18″ × 60″

A collage is built on a base fabric, through the addition and subtraction of your design elements, guided by the principles of composition. The bulk of my time is spent auditioning, layering, creating relationships, switching out, and narrowing down, until I find that just-right magical composition that makes it all sing in harmony.

I may be biased, but I find collage quilting to be the most relaxing, fun, gratifying, and easy method of quilting. In her 1970 book, *Quilts and Coverlets: A Contemporary Approach*, Jean Ray Laury called it the *applied top method*, "in which you start out with a full-sized fabric base to which you add design elements." It allows for a mixed-media approach, combining media and materials such as drawing, painting, machine stitching, stamping, mark making, and more to the base fabric before, while, or after applying your photo(s) and fabric elements. This collage or applied top method of working does not preclude using piecing to create the base fabric or any of the layers. The base of my quilt *Lineage* (page 65) is pieced, and some of the layers in *California Dreamer* (page 71) are pieced— design decisions I made that furthered the story I was telling.

The collage is built from the bottom up, consisting of several overlapping layers. Right about now, you may be thinking, "Wait, doesn't she have to take it all apart in order to stitch it all together?" The answer is no. That would be crazy and time-consuming, wouldn't it? I came up with a very workable solution I have been using since I made my first *Fragment* collages back in 1999. I call it the *top down* method of appliqué. I use Mistyfuse, a paperless fusible web.

Appliqué the Top Down Way

1. Pin as you layer your fabrics, if necessary or desired, depending on size and positioning.

2. Lift the fabric layers around the edges, to insert enough fusible web (Mistyfuse) to keep things in place. Think of it as tacking down the fabric prior to stitching.

3. Iron to fuse.

4. Starting with the uppermost fabric or photo, stitch in place. This will secure the underlying layers, too. I use and recommend a walking foot or similar foot, to prevent the layers from shifting.

5. Working toward the base fabric, continue to stitch the edges of the subsequent layers onto the underlying and/or

Peel back layers to insert fusible web.

background fabrics. Not every edge has to be stitched; it's an art quilt. Loose edges create depth and movement.

Text Talk

Adding text or words may be an integral part of your story: an old recipe, a handwritten letter, dates and names, and other details. Some text-based items can be photographed and printed or transferred directly onto the fabric. Adding text in a variety of ways will enrich the surface. How many ways can you get words onto your quilt? Here's a list of 13 methods that I have used.

Samples of printed and written text in a variety of fonts

PRINTED ON FABRIC

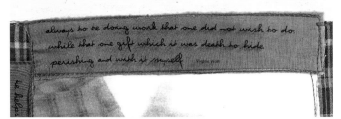

Text printed directly onto fabric; detail from *The Apron* (page 8)

HANDWRITTEN

Handwritten story in permanent marker

TRANSFERRED

Photographed and TAP-transferred signature from *Lineage* (page 65)

STENCILED

MACHINE-EMBROIDERED TEXT

FREE-MOTION WRITING

HAND-STITCHED TEXT

PREPRINTED ON COMMERCIAL FABRIC

THERMOFAX SCREENED

SCREENPRINTED

DISCHARGED

STAMPED

Large stamps for important words

CUT FROM A BOOK AND EITHER GLUED OR BACKED WITH FUSIBLE WEB AND STITCHED

Snippet of text from an old book, glued onto fabric

What have I missed?

Special Effects

Work of sight is done. Now do heart work on the pictures within you.
— RAINER MARIA RILKE —

Punched holes on TAP paper before transfer allows the pink silk fabric to show through. Backed with pink silk, three-dimensional fabric paint on crown, and an errant thread from the silk placed around the neck and fused into the TAP polymer after the transfer

I've been printing and using edited and/or manipulated photos as-is for over twenty years. There's really no need to do anything else to your photos. But may I tempt you with these extras? Sometimes a photo, or a story, just needs a little embellishment. Consider these:

- Drawing on the photo
- Hand coloring the photo
- Stitching onto the photo
- Adding collage to the photo
- Subtracting with cutouts, punches, burns

Water-soluble pencils were used to color this black-and-white TAP-transferred photo.

- Cutting the photo apart

Large TAP transfer cut into squares and stitched to base fabric

- Thread Painting

Award-winning quilter and thread painter with mad skills, Nanette S. Zeller, applied her skills to a sketch of Civil War nurse Helen Louise Gilson. I created the sketch with an app and printed the image onto fabric, and Nanette thread painted the shawl and hand colored the gloves using a colored pencils set with screen-printing extender.

Thread painting and details by Nanette S. Zeller

Finishing & Display

Quilt Finishing

Now that the story is told, what will the ending be? That depends on your end goals and your quilting aesthetics. You may desire a traditional finish and appearance, or perhaps you will give one of my artsy methods a try. Maybe you are interested in alternative ways to finish your quilt.

While you are the bearer of the memory, the creator and designer of your memory quilt, you may also have to take into consideration how and where this quilt will be displayed. Some shows have strict rules on finishing that you need to follow to enter. Art galleries may welcome your artful finishes with open arms. If you are creating for another person, the recipient may be traditional-minded and not understand your "artful" finish. Others may appreciate your personal approach. As creators, we are not supposed to care what *they* think. It takes a strong sense of artistic self to not care what others think, especially because we do want our quilts to be seen and our work appreciated. Do not stifle your creativity because of what *they* might think. Follow your heart and artistic sensibility. It is what sets you and your quilt apart from the crowd.

Quilting

I believe that we should create in service to the art. In my experience, I know when a quilt deserves a formal finish and when it can take a more artful approach. I'm neither a rebel quilter nor a perfectionist. I approach my quilts as art held together by stitching. The actual quilting of a quilt is not high on my list. (Is that blasphemous?) I would rather put my time into designing another quilt.

The quilting line creates shape, space, movement, and texture, and follows the principles of pattern, repetition, and unity. How you quilt your quilt should be a decision made early on during the composition of the quilt top. For example, quilting lines and batting selection can create depth, which may be important to your story. If the quilting is to be decorative and you want it to be noticed, be sure that it adds to and does not draw attention away from the message and meaning.

Basic quilting lines to hold the quilt sandwich together may be all that is necessary, especially when working on a smaller quilt. A collage quilt top will have a lot of separate elements, and an overall quilting pattern may not be practical. Consider how you can add quilting in ways that can enhance the story—such as tying, to emphasize ties to family or to a special place. What about hand quilting all or some of the quilt sections? Whatever you decide, do what makes *you* feel best and makes your quilt look better.

Binding

Binding your quilt can continue to add to the story or quietly end it, depending on the finish you choose.

Binding a quilt began as a utilitarian way to prolong its life. Traditionally, a quilt is bound with a separate piece of fabric that serves to enclose the batting and neatly finish the edges of the quilt. The binding had to be easy to remove and replace when the quilt edges became worn and frayed with use. Today that is rarely an issue. Quilters have the freedom to finish quilt edges in a variety of both unnoticeable and decorative ways.

The standard binding is still an excellent way to finish your quilt, but we now have the freedom to use new ways to finish (or not!) the edges of your quilt. Let me present you with a few other options to consider.

Fused Strips or Squares Finish

A playful fused zigzag binding

Package-Fold Finish

Package-fold with decorative stitching

This variation uses a fusible web instead of stitching. Trim to even the edges of your finished but unbound quilt. Iron a fusible web to the back of your chosen binding fabric. Cut binding strips to the full length of each edge of your quilt and 2 times as wide as you want the finished binding to be *plus a bit extra depending on the thickness of your quilt.* Fold the strips in half lengthwise over the quilt edge and iron to bond.

For a decorative zigzag look, cut squares 1½″ × 1½″, or larger, depending on the size of your quilt and desired appearance, from fabric backed with fusible web. Wrap the squares over the binding to create triangles. Iron to fuse to the quilt, overlapping the endpoints of the triangles as you go. Add a straight or decorative stitch if desired.

This is a simple and timesaving finishing method that uses the quilt backing to create a finished quilt edge and border at the same time. It is one of my favorite methods and I use it for my collage quilts. Choose a backing fabric that will complement and frame the quilt top. Cut or piece a backing the size of your quilt plus the size of the border you desire, plus 2″ extra to extend under the quilt top. Cut the batting to the size of the quilt top plus the width of the border.

Lay the backing fabric right side down. Place the batting on top. Fold the 2 long sides toward the quilt center. Press. Fold the ends of the short sides at a 45° angle, as if you were wrapping a package. Fold the mitered ends toward the quilt center, and press the fold and the sides. Trim any excess bulk. Place the quilt top over the folded edges of the quilt backing. Baste the quilt top and border and quilt as desired.

A package-fold finish revealed

Pillowcase Finish

Detail of *Family Garden* (page 6), with pillowcase finish

This method both provides a surface for collage quilting and finishes the quilt edges. It is quite a time-saver. Choose the quilt top fabric and cut it to the desired size, plus a ¼″ seam allowance all around. Cut the backing fabric to the same size as the quilt top. Layer your quilt top and backing fabric, right sides together. Add a layer of thin batting on top of the quilt top and backing. (I use Warm & Natural or felt.) Stitch around the edges, leaving an opening large enough to turn the quilt sandwich right side out. Trim the seam allowance at the corners at a 45° angle. Turn the quilt right side out, smoothing the edges and defining the corners with a wooden spoon handle or similar object. Hand stitch the opening closed.

≈ TIP ≈

The "pillowcase" can be also be created first and then used as the base for a quilt collage. Collage your photos, fabric, and embellishments on the quilt top and machine or hand stitch through all the layers as you go. When you take your final stitch, your quilt is complete!

Faced Finish

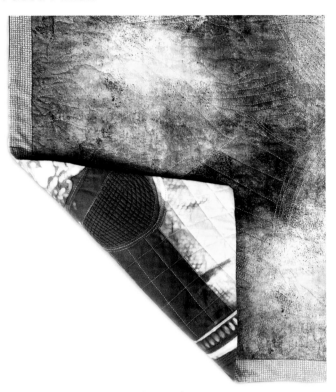

Faced finish on *Ten of Cups* (page 38)

A facing (or faced binding) is similar to a binding on a quilt, except that the facing fabric is sewn to the quilt sandwich edges and then entirely turned to the back, so the facing is not seen from the front. It is considered a more artful finish. There are a variety of ways to accomplish a faced finish, with several tutorials and videos available online. Contributor Susan Brubaker Knapp has made an art of the faced binding finish. I recommend the two excellent facing tutorials on her website (See Contributors (page 126).

Trimmed Felt Edge

A zigzag felt edge adds a playful finish to this quilt.

Use felt as both your quilt batting and backing? Yes! Using only two layers is acceptable in an art or memory quilt. Measure and cut a piece of felt the dimensions of your quilt top plus the amount of felt border you want showing, plus 3″ extra. Center, baste, and quilt your quilt top on the felt. Optionally, if it is a small quilt, square the quilt and stitch the quilt top edges to attach it to the felt. Use a zigzag or scallop rotary cutter to trim the felt edges.

No Finish

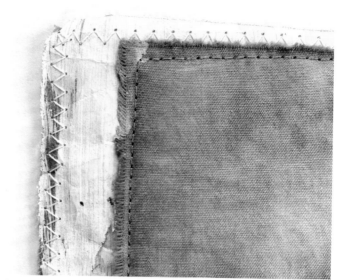

This unfinished edge enhances and adds to the overall story of the materials and quilt.

In this case, not finishing the edges is the finish! Trim your batting so it lies inside the edges of the quilt top. Sew around the raw edges of your quilt sandwich to secure the layers.

Trimmed Satin or Zigzag Stitch Finish

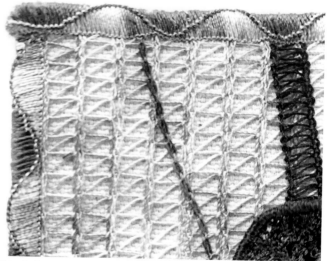

Detail of *The Chickadee* (page 108) by Michelle Umlauf
Quilt bound with decorative satin stitch using variegated thread

Using a satin stitch, or a looser zigzag stitch, sew ¼″ from the edges of the quilt sandwich. Trim the excess fabric close to the outer edge of the sewn stitching, being careful not to cut the stitches.

Sign & Personalize

A quilt is not finished until you sign it. How you do that is up to you. It can be as simple as your name and date in permanent marker on the back, or …

- your hand-embroidered signature
- a custom-designed, machine embroidered label
- a description of the story behind the quilt
- a charming token on hand-stitched and bound fabric

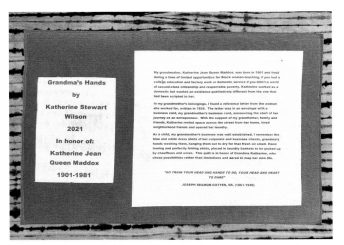

Katherine Stewart Wilson added a label and a story about her grandmother on her quilt back.

A small hand-stitched fabric square provides a frame for the heart charm and Linda Trenholm's signature on the back.

Michelle Umlauf personalized the back of her quilt with a machine-embroidered chickadee print and her grandmother's photo.

Display

There are a variety of options for displaying your photo memory quilt. There are three primary factors you need to consider when deciding on a display option.

WHO IS THE QUILT FOR?

If the quilt is a personal memory or created just for you, anything goes, even stacking it away in your completed projects pile (although I hope you display and admire it, at least for a while). If it is for a family member or close friend, discuss it with them before or after you present it to them. If it is a commission, it is likely you have already discussed display with your client.

WILL IT BE FORMALLY DISPLAYED?

Where your quilt will hang will determine how you finish and display it. If you think you might enter it in a quilt show, then you will need to comply with the sleeve and hanging requirements. An art exhibit may prefer that it be mounted on stretcher bars or attached to a canvas. Small quilts that you intend to display and sell in a craft shop setting will have the most lenient rules, and an atypical or eye-catching display might lead to a sale.

Detail of *The Weavers* (page 83), mounted on fabric-covered 14″ × 18″ cradled board

HOW LARGE IS IT?

These are my recommendations based on my experience of displaying quilts, not hard-and-fast rules.

Less than 24″ on each side: Frame or mount it on canvas or a cradled panel. Grouping with other small works will have a greater visual impact. Consider using …

- small clear plastic rings, one on each corner of the top
- a vintage or new wooden clamp-type slacks hanger
- black or DIY painted binder clips

Larger than 48″ on each side: At this size, a quilt can hold its own hanging on a wall. Depending on its weight, consider adding …

- a sleeve on the back
- hook-and-loop tape
- fishing line and wooden slat
- tabs for a curtain/drapery rod or a large branch
- painted dowel with wooden craft finials
- coordinating fabric-covered dowel
- commercial quilt hangers

From 24″ to 48″ on each side: Use either of the previous options or a combination of both.

A vintage wooden hanger is a convenient changeable display option. Quilt by Gina Louthian-Stanley (page 124).

PROJECTS

I love sharing and demystifying my process. I don't have any right or wrong ways of working to share, just what works for me and has worked for me for twenty-plus years. Take what you can use, or work in a manner that you are comfortable or familiar with. I don't expect you to follow my projects step by step. How could you? You are not going to re-create my memory. Everything presented in these projects is intended as a guide. I am bringing my memories to life, and you have your own memories to work with and your own stories to tell. I walk you through my process to help you to better grasp and understand all the techniques and information I have shared up to this point. Following along with my process will give you ideas, insight, and inspiration when you begin to create your photo memory quilt. Here's to many Aha! moments.

Lineage

Finished size: 30″ × 60″

Photo by C&T Publishing

When I was young, my dad told me that his ancestor, Ninian Beall, used to own all of Georgetown, a tree-lined neighborhood in the northwest section of Washington, D.C. It was once home to more than 40 tribes of Native Americans, and it grew northward from its site on the Potomac River as an early pre-Revolutionary War shipping port into what is now a tony neighborhood of historic homes and row houses dating back to the 1700s. Even though I was young, I took my dad's assertion with a grain of salt—family lore grown out of proportion over the years.

Thanks to modern methods of ancestral research, I was proved wrong! The story sounds like the basis for the *Outlander* series. Born in 1625 in Scotland, Beall spent the first 27 years of his life living out scenes similar to those in the books and TV series. A redhead standing 6′7″ tall, Beall was taken prisoner while fighting in the Scottish Army at the Battle of Dunbar. He landed in a London prison, and shortly thereafter, he and 149 other prisoners were shipped to the island of Barbados in the West Indies to live as indentured servants. In 1652, Beall entered into another five-year indentured servant arrangement in Maryland. Once free, over the years, Ninian Beall patented and owned more than 15,000 acres of Maryland, a portion of it now the part of Washington, D.C. known as Georgetown. It was parceled and sold over the years, but most of the original mansions built by Beall's descendants, including Dumbarton Oaks, are still standing and considered historic sites.

Fast-forward a few generations. Ninian's story explains my great-great-grandfather, Richard Plummer Jackson's interest in Georgetown and his subsequent book *The Chronicles of Georgetown*, written in 1878 and dedicated to his son, William (Willie) S. Jackson, my great-grandfather. And that brings us to my grandfather, Leslie Hall Jackson, and my father, Leslie Hall Jackson, Jr., a member of the Greatest Generation, shot down over Austria in WWII on October 9, 1942. He was captured by the enemy and spent the rest of the war as a POW. Sound familiar?

To round out the story, Ninian Beall had the names of both a Christian saint and a Druid priest. History has it that he was likely descended from the Celts. In the fourth century BC, a division of the northern Celts called the Picts settled in Fife, Scotland. Ninian's father was born in Fifeshire, Scotland. The Celts relied on the ministry of the Druids, and the Druid priests became known by the name Beall. I take all of this with a grain of salt, but it has been well researched by others.

I used public domain images of a Druid priest, St. Ninian, and a Pict woman warrior to represent the earliest part of my lineage. I am honored to be a descendant of such a strong family line and was compelled to create this as a visual memory for my 6 children, 16 grandchildren, and generations to come.

Note: Andrew Jackson Beall was the father of Martha Ann (Mattie) Beall, who married my great-grandfather, William Jackson. Their portrait is to the left of my dad's POW photo, just above the photograph of my father's parents.

MATERIALS

A selection of 15 edited and restored photographs printed on TAP Transfer Artist Paper and transferred to cotton fabric

A selection of 10 fabrics that spoke to me of the past and the times when each generation lived

Fusible web (I used Mistyfuse.)

Parchment paper

Additional fabric snippets to frame images

Backing fabric

Batting (I used an 80/20 blend.)

Optional: Embroidery module

≥ PARCHMENT, PLEASE ≤

When ironing fusible web onto the back of TAP-transferred photos, *always* place the image with the transferred side facing down onto parchment paper before ironing. Since the heat will soften the transfer, making it adhere to the ironing surface, using parchment paper will keep the transfer clean. The parchment paper is easily removed after the fusible is applied. If you are using a paperless fusible, like Mistyfuse, also place a piece of parchment paper over the fusible.

Method

Starting with a rough sketch of my envisioned design, my first step was to determine the size and placement of the fabric strips and the photographs. I laid out the fabrics in the desired order and proportions prior to cutting. I created a ¼″-scale drawing as a guide for fabric cutting and preliminary photo sizing.

The strips were machine pieced. Once I had the background complete, I could audition the photographs and determine the best size for each. I did this first with black-and-white photos printed on paper.

Once I finalized the photo sizes, I made a small test print and transfers of all the images using 2 sheets of TAP transfer paper to check the color, contrast, and brightness of each image. Tweaks were made to satisfy what was in my mind's eye and I printed the images full size.

Before trimming the printed images, fusible web was applied to the back of each image.

The images were pinned in place to determine the final layout. Once I finalized the layout, I brought in other fabrics to help define and bring the images forward from the background, where necessary.

With everything in place, I fused the photos to the background, adding any additional fusible necessary to hold fabric snippets in place. I stitched all the photos in place prior to quilting.

I made a quilt sandwich with the quilt top, a layer of batting, and backing fabric and pin basted prior to quilting.

Using a walking foot and beginning at the middle of the quilt, I quilted evenly spaced horizontal lines to reinforce the lineage concept of the quilt. (I did not quilt the photographs.)

I then machine stitched a faced finish (page 59) to the quilt top edges, turned, pressed, and hand stitched it on the back.

As a final embellishment and way to record them for posterity, the names of each of my known ancestors were machine embroidered and fused to the respective images.

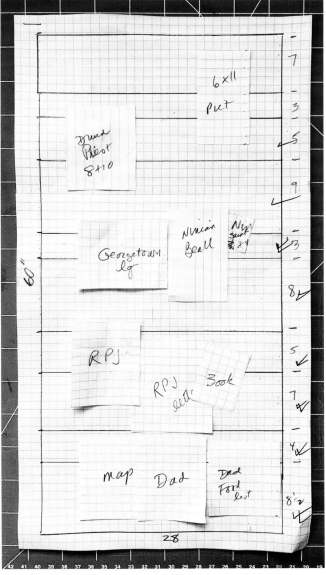

Initial to-scale drawing for pieced fabric strips and photo sizes

Cyano Anna

Finished size: 35″ × 43″

Photo by C&T Publishing

According to Wikipedia, English botanist and photographer Anna Atkins is "considered the first person to publish a book illustrated with photographic images. Some sources say that she was the first woman to create a photograph." She hand-made only two books, *Photographs of British Algae: Cyanotype Impressions* and *Cyanotypes of British and Foreign Plants and Ferns*, both in 1843. They have been preserved, reprinted commercially, and honored with museum exhibitions.

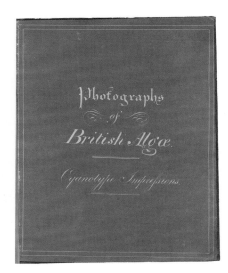

Cover page from book of cyanotype prints by Anna Atkins (public domain)

My creative time is dictated by the seasons. Fall and winter are for indoor quilting. When spring rolls around, heralding the time when the sun is higher and hotter, my attention turns to cyanotype printing. I have acquired quite a stash of cyanotype prints. Writing this book was the impetus to finally make a quilt with these lovelies. I wanted to pay homage to the woman who created the first book of photographs. Cyanotype is a cameraless photographic process.

MATERIALS

Cyanotype solution

Natural-fiber fabrics

Prepared-for-printing, paper-backed fabric for photo

Additional coordinating nature prints and fabrics to intersperse with cyanotype prints

Backing board (cardboard) sized to fit cyanotype fabrics

Glass to cover fabric for exposure

Leaves for printing (You can also use lace, feathers, cutouts, or any other relatively flat items.)

Water for rinsing

A sunny day

Backing fabric

Batting (I used Warm & Natural.)

Design and placement of the fabrics

Method

I drew from my collection of cyanotype prints, choosing ones that would vary in size, color (shade), and fabric, to provide variety and interest.

I began by laying out the prints and coordinating fabrics to form the quilt top, keeping the elements and principles of composition in mind.

This is the part of the process I truly enjoy, so I was well into it before I realized that I had no background fabric in place. I solved my dilemma by piecing the quilt top in sections. The size I was working at made getting a good perspective on the proportions and placement for the overall composition difficult, so I took a lot of photos along the way to assist me. I highly suggest you use a background fabric when doing your layout.

Piecing the quilt in sections

With everything in place and pieced or layered and stitched together, it was time to work out the size and placement of the Anna Atkins photograph. I didn't want her portrait image to draw too much attention and become the focal point, only for it to be a meaningful contribution to the overall patterning and composition. I printed out several different-size images on paper, added several filters and adjustments to tone down the color (see Tempering App Fever, page 29), and arrived at one I thought was subtle and blended well. The photo was printed on paper-backed fabric for printing.

NOTE ℗ *The original public domain image was in black and white, so I initially colorized it to lessen the attention-drawing contrast with the overall blue of the quilt.*

I layered the completed quilt top with batting and backing fabric, and pin basted it in place in preparation for quilting. I echo quilted around each image.

The quilt is finished with a machine stitched faced binding on the edges and hand stitched on the back.

California Dreamer

Photo by C&T Publishing

Smitten with the photograph a friend posted on Instagram of her redheaded mother, I asked my friend if I could use it for a quilt. My first book, *Quilted Memories,* also had a quilt inspired by a student's photo of her redheaded mother. (I think I have a thing for redheads.) Mary Ellen Small, aka Molly, struck me as a woman with presence and determination. I wanted to convey that sense by removing the background and enlarging the figure in the original 5″ × 7″ photo, so it would dominate the quilt. Adding the bright floral fabric as the background was an instant decision, and I was excited that it did indeed add to, but not overpower, Molly's presence.

To ensure that the figure of Molly always retained dominance and emphasis, I decided to have a second print made of just the figure, that I would slightly pad to elevate it from the background. I erased the background from my digital image of the original in Photoshop and added this new image to the full yard of fabric I was having printed. (Actually, I had a total of three figures printed since there was room on the one-yard piece. I wanted to have a backup just in case, and something for a future project.)

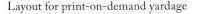

Layout for print-on-demand yardage

I asked my friend for some details and background on her mother to help me create a story and integrate her story into my design. She provided me with major highlights and facts, but in the telling, much emotion was revealed. I used what I thought were the most memorable and salient points, and translated them into visuals for this narrative memory quilt. I also got to raid my stash of ephemera and embellishments. It all just felt like something Molly would approve of. In a nod to Molly's love of pastels, I created pieced blocks to surround the figure and act as a bridge between the soft colors she always wore and the bright, deeply saturated, attention-getting colors of the background fabric I chose.

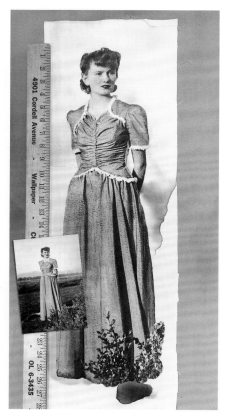

The test-painted, enlarged figure with the original photo for comparison

MATERIALS

Enlarged photo plus an additional image of just the figure, printed-on-demand

Background fabrics chosen for scale, theme, and color to give dominance to the figure

Fusible web (I used Mistyfuse.)

Midweight interfacing

Squares, 6″ to 14″, of bleached muslin for painting

Vintage collage elements (birds, butterflies, a chicken) printed on TAP Transfer Artist Paper and transferred to fabric

Fluid acrylics (I used Golden Artist Colors.)

Foam brush, 2″

Styrofoam plate for paint

Backing fabric

Batting

Floral embellishments from my stash

Optional: Inktense pencils

Method

I added minimal hand painting to the isolated figure image to add dimension and make the color pop, prior to cutting it out.

I applied fusible to the back of the solo figure, prior to trimming it from the background. I cut the figure away from the background fabric, leaving a 1″ margin for turning under.

To further emphasize the figure, I used interfacing to give it more heft and presence. I traced the figure edges onto the interfacing (by taping both to my patio door window) and cut the interfacing to the size and shape of the figure. I clipped the edges and curves of the figure's turn-under allowance, turned it under toward the back of the interfacing, and ironed to fuse it in place.

To create the pastel quilt blocks, I taped large cotton fabric squares to the dull side of freezer paper and painted them with diluted washes of fluid acrylics to match the pastel colors Molly loved to wear. I cut and stitched blocks together in 2- and 4"-square units.

With all the elements in place, it was time to decide how much and at what point of the horizon to join the floral background fabric to the sky background fabric. I wanted the figure grounded and standing in her "roots," with a magical, exciting "sky" suggesting her future—her California dreams. I chose the proportions I wanted for the 2 background fabrics and stitched them together.

I chose the final placement of the detached figure by aligning it with her location on the lower background fabric. The pastel-painted blocks were arranged and added behind the figure for interest, variety, and a nod to Molly. I fused the figure and blocks to the background.

I found copyright-free images of a chicken, some butterflies, and hummingbirds (Molly's favorite), and edited and resized the images. I printed them onto TAP paper, backed them with fusible web, and trimmed each one. I trimmed additional elements from leftover background fabric, added fusible, and trimmed them to shape. These elements helped tie the background to the foreground and unite the top print fabric with the lower portion of the photograph. I added additional color to some of the elements with water-soluble Inktense pencils to saturate the color.

Then it was time to audition all the story elements I had gathered. Going through them all, I easily chose those I knew I would definitely use and eliminated others as not being relevant. I reserved just a few for possible inclusion. I didn't want the quilt to be too busy or crowded, not that anything could steal the show from Molly. As always, I was guided by my desire to create a meaningful and cohesive story and composition.

I finalized the placement of all the chosen elements and photographed the quilt top, so any disturbed items could be repositioned after the top was at the sewing machine. I fused everything but the dimensional flowers in place.

I layered the quilt top with batting and a muslin backing, and machine quilted it with a walking foot. I squared the sandwich, and trimmed and layered it with a backing fabric to create a pillowcase finish (page 59). I hand stitched the opening closed.

I added the final flower embellishments and beads by hand.

Glory Be

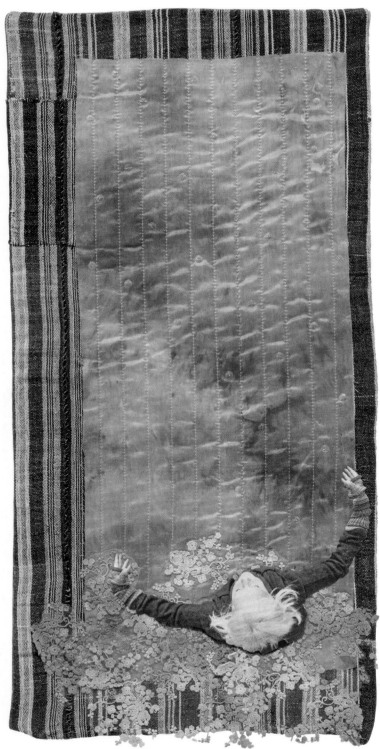

Photo by C&T Publishing

This quilt was a long time coming. I had the original concept for *Glory* Be almost ten years before it came to fruition. It captures the very visceral memory of the first sunset I experienced on the day we moved to a farm in 2012. Unpacking in the kitchen, I glanced up and out the window, and saw the most beautiful colors in the sky. I ran outside and literally fell to my knees in awe. Having lived inside the Washington, D.C., Beltway all my life, the expanse and magnificent color show put on by the sunset over the open fields was a first for me and brought tears to my eyes. My husband was still at the other house, so I had no one to share this moment with but God. That feeling still stays with me—a very personal and deep memory.

So how did I get a photograph of that moment? I didn't. A few months (a year?) later, I asked my husband to shoot a photo of me, from above, arms outstretched, for another quilt I had in mind. That, too, got sidetracked. What you see here is a scaled-down version of my original vision, imbued with the beauty of my snow-dyed fabrics and the lasting emotion of that original moment. The love and appreciation of beautiful sunsets is universal. I hope some of the emotion I felt that day, September 11, 2012, makes its way into your heart.

MATERIALS

Photo printed on TAP Transfer Artist Paper and transferred to cotton fabric

Fusible web (I used Mistyfuse.)

Snow-dyed silk/cotton blend fabric

Snow-dyed commercial embroidery

Scrap of vintage African indigo fabric

Basting glue (I used Roxanne Glue-Baste-It.)

Backing fabric

Batting

Clear sequins

The original, larger image I started with, contrasted with the smaller one in this quilt. It is overlaid on one of the sunsets that inspired me.

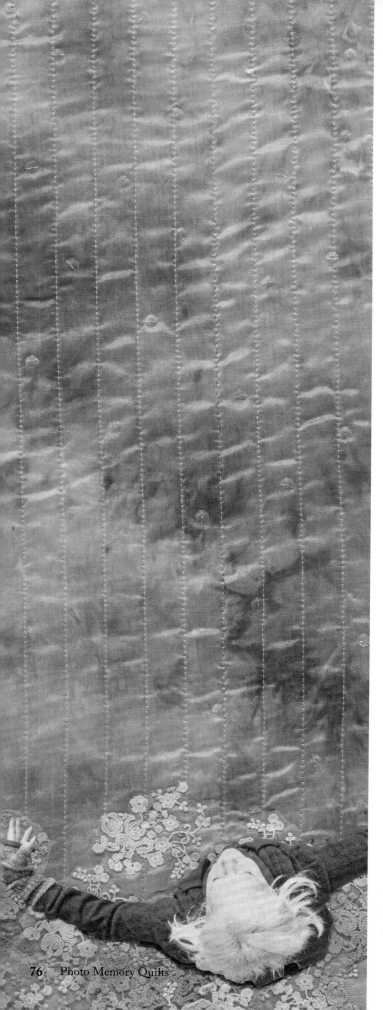

Method

After searching for (and finding!) the UFO project and the arms-outstretched photograph my husband took years ago, I turned to my stash to find a fabric that would convey the splendor of that sunset and project the concepts of radiance and heaven. I could have gone bright, chromatic, and dramatic, but I kept returning to the soft orange/blue of snow-dyed silk/cotton blend fabric. After auditioning several fabrics to serve as a base for the silky sky, I settled on a woven, hand-pieced, striped remnant of vintage African indigo. It reminded me of the color of the sky that follows the sunset. It had a well-worn frayed area, which I hand-repaired as a nod to the hand stitching present in the fabric.

Fusible web was applied to the back of the TAP transfer and was trimmed. A 2˝ piece of fusible was ironed onto the short side of the upper portion of the length of silk/cotton blend. By fusing just this portion of the silk/cotton in place to the background fabric, I was able to smooth the length of silk/cotton tautly to pin and hand baste it in place prior to quilting.

I machine quilted it using a walking foot, working from the center to the edges, enabling the silk to shimmer downward.

I trimmed the snow-dyed embroidery and selectively glued it to the base of the silk and down to the front edge. The quilt will not be wetted or washed, so the basting glue will hold. (I chose it for its fine applicator tip.) A sheer black fabric shadow was fused to the bottom edge of the TAP transferred image which was fused and glued, not stitched, in place.

The indigo remnant had a lovely rolled hem edge at the bottom that I wanted to retain. I made a layered quilt sandwich of top, batting, and backing in preparation for a pillowcase finish (page 59). I stitched 3 sides, leaving the bottom open so I could fold in the backing fabric and hand stitch the opening closed, allowing the rolled edge and embroidery to have a more organic feel and appearance.

I thought I was done, but it just needed something more. I always tend toward the subtle, so luckily, I found some clear sequins in my stash. I hand stitched the sequins in place using a silver metallic thread. They provided just the glimmer of sunlight I needed.

Clara Barton

For over 50 years I lived just three miles from the home of Clara Barton, founder of the American Red Cross. Built in 1891, it was first used primarily as a Red Cross warehouse until 1897, when it became Barton's personal residence; it remained so until she died in 1912 at the age of 90. The house then served as the first headquarters for the Red Cross, became a National Historic Landmark in 1965, and was opened to visitors about the time of my first visit in 1966.

I was too young to fully understand who this remarkable woman was and all that she accomplished in her long life. It wasn't until 2020, when I became interested in the actions of citizens during the Civil War, that I learned her story and the details of her unrelenting service to Americans. First a teacher, then a nurse in the Civil War, Barton became known as the Angel of the Battlefield. After her war service opened her eyes to the great need, she established the American Red Cross. She also opened a Missing Soldiers Office in Washington, D.C., after the war, to help families find their lost loved ones. This quilt is my tribute to her accomplishments and memory, and my strong personal connections to the location.

This detail from the quilt shows a lot of the little details that help tell the story.

My favorite Clara Barton anecdote ties her to the adjacent Glen Echo Park, an amusement park I frequented as a child. When the house was her residence, the park manager wanted to turn it into a hotel. Barton refused, so he proceeded to build the park around it, hoping to force her out. He installed a Ferris wheel and scenic train ride tracks right in front of her house. It didn't work. Barton wrote in her diary, "The evenings are very pretty—the lights cheerful. The noise in no way Disturbs us." You can see a photo of her house and those tracks under the red cross on the quilt.

MATERIALS

Selected photos

TAP Transfer Artist Paper

Cotton organdy and black linen for photo transfers

Vintage textiles from my collection

Hand-dyed wool for cross

Antique quilt block

Old book cover

Vintage metal ephemera

Batting (I used Warm & Natural.)

Felt for backing

Method

I began with a layered background of 2 antique textiles from my stash. I always knew that the hemmed organdy piece with the red cross that I purchased many years ago would come in handy one day.

Two photos were transferred onto organdy, which I chose because of its similarity to bandages. The black linen was chosen to frame the portrait and to set it apart from the background. It also provided balance with the row of the repeated element, the Missing Soldiers Office sign, transferred directly onto the black linen using white paint on the TAP prior to transfer. See my book *The Ultimate Guide to Transfer Artist Paper* (C&T Publishing), for more details on this technique. To make the face more prominent, I placed a layer of batting behind it and stitched below the chin to create depth.

I placed additional stained organdy behind Barton's photo to add depth, texture, and movement. An old sash, stained with age and folded in the form of a ribbon banner, is a nod to her accomplishments and serves to add diagonals and dimensionality.

I placed a late 1800s Nine-Patch quilt block with a central red cross below and beneath the portrait. Beneath the quilt block lies an old cloth book cover (removed from the book board), used to create an interesting edge and, again, add movement and variety to the composition. The faded, age-stained red reminds us of the wear and tear and destruction that occurred during the war.

I seed stitched a red wool cross onto a rust-stained, linen fragment with raw edges. I then machine stitched the fragment to another linen scrap, leaving the frayed edge visible to indicate age, create movement, and soften the rectangular forms. I machine stitched the completed element to the other layers. Finally, I backed the photo of Barton's house with batting to create depth and improve the contrast of the image, then stitched it to the quilt top.

A small scrap of vintage fabric in brighter colors plus a touch of fiber is held in place by the stitching around the house photo. It is an element important to the composition. It creates a pop of color not found in this black, white, and red quilt. Left unstitched, it creates movement, and its shape both balances the diagonal of the house photo and leads the eye down to the row of signs. The middle areas of interest cause the viewer's eyes not just to bounce back and forth from Barton's face to the black line, but instead to pause and linger at the variety of elements in between.

To create the finish, I squared and trimmed the quilt top to 22″ × 32″. I placed the quilt top on batting, cut to the finished size of 20″ × 30″. I folded 1″ of the quilt top edges over the batting and ironed them in place with the corners mitered. I cut a piece of felt 19½″ × 29½″, centered it over the quilt back, and pinned it in place. I stitched the layers together around the perimeter, ¼″ from the outer edge.

Modified self-faced quilt finish with felt backing

Last, I added 2 antique metal Red Cross embellishments with glue.

High Rock: Then & Now

Finished size: 19½″ × 23″

After most of a lifetime as a city girl, in 2015 my husband and I moved to a small mountain town, just a block from the Maryland-Pennsylvania state line, also known as the Mason-Dixon Line, and home to Pen Mar Park. In 1877, Pen Mar Amusement Park was created by a railroad owner who wanted to extend his line and transport city dwellers to the cool, mountain-air resorts in the summertime. The original train station is just down the hill from us and is now a library. By the turn of the last century, the Pen Mar area had become one of the most popular resort destinations in the eastern United States. It's all gone now, except for the parkland and scenic High Rock, one of the original attractions.

We discovered it by accident while driving around our new neighborhood. Now we take family and visitors there, and occasionally escape our home offices to visit when we are in need of wide-open, majestic views. The site is now covered with graffiti, which, in my eye, makes it an even more delightful, definitely colorful, experience. But it's the views that melt my heart. From an artistic and compositional point of view, it is the juxtaposition of those 2 elements that makes it an engaging, inspiring, and art-filled experience.

When we moved to the mountain, I scoured the internet for vintage postcards of the area to frame and hang in the entry, so I already had the images I needed to flesh out this quilt. You can usually find antique and vintage postcards of your location at antique stores and online. The large central image was in the public domain and downloaded from the internet. Family photos provided the "now." Together they create a lasting memory of a location and a family.

MATERIALS

Vintage location postcards	Base fabric
Photographs from a family visit	Backing fabric
TAP Transfer Artist Paper	Batting (I used Warm & Natural.)
White cotton fabric for TAP transfers	
Fusible web	

Cumberland Valley from High Rock, Pen Mar, Pa.

22-4

Contrasting the old view from the antique High Rock postcard with the current view in a change of seasons

RYLAND R.R. — PEN-MAR REGION — BEAUTIES OF THE BLUE RIDGE.

Method

I always start with photos printed on paper to determine the size and eventual layout; that way, if I have too many photos, or not enough, I don't waste TAP paper. Here, after sizing and color-checking all the photographs, I printed them onto TAP and transferred them onto white cotton. I ironed fusible to the back of the images prior to trimming.

I chose to use the large central vintage image as an anchor and resting point for the eye as it travels around to the other 10 images. Retaining the vintage sepia color offers contrast with the color images and emphasizes the juxtaposition between then and now.

The background fabric is an on-demand print made from a photograph of a pile of hand-painted and indigo-dipped papers. It provided the blue sky, earth, and rocky tones and appearance I needed.

I chose a package-fold finish (page 58) for this quilt and prepared the backing and batting, creating the mitered and turned-in edges/border. I fused the quilt top with the fused images onto the backing and stitched around the perimeter. I stitched the fused images in place through all layers. The quilt was complete. This was a quick and easy way to capture the memory.

The Weavers

Finished size: 14″ × 18″

Inspired by the public domain photograph of two women posing with their shuttles, I wanted to create an homage to their time working in the mill. I sourced an antique shuttle online and knew that I would need a sturdy way to mount it. To determine the size of the mounting, first I needed to create the quilt that would be the focal point.

Fabrics that were woven, or appeared to be, were chosen for this piece.

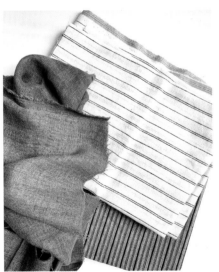

Woven fabrics chosen for the quilt

MATERIALS

Photo printed on inkjet-ready fabric

Assorted fabrics for quilt layers

Background fabric to cover cradled board

Glue for fabric (I used Talas Jade 403 PVA Adhesive; archival glue for fabric.)

Fusible web

Squeegee or old credit card

Batting (I used Warm & Natural.)

Polyester stuffing (I used Poly-fil.)

Embroidery thread and needle

Beads for fastening quilt layers and embellishment

14″ × 18″ cradled board

Carpet tape

Vintage weaving shuttle

Wood glue and C-clamps

Small brass frame

Method

The quilt is composed of 2 quiltlets: a bottom layer, which forms a frame for the top layer, which consists of an antique image printed onto fabric. Both layers were made with the Pillowcase finish (see page 59).

I machine quilted the top layer, stitching around the image of the two weavers. I wanted to give more definition to the heads than the quilting provided, so I slashed the back of the quiltlet and used the trapunto technique to add polyester stuffing to raise the heads. I added a running stitch under the chins to provide further definition and dimension. I also added seed beads as buttons on the clothing.

I quilted the bottom layer with embroidery thread using a cross-stitch.

I attached the top layer to the bottom layer with beads at the corners. I sandwiched 2 complementary fabric swatches and fused them between the quiltlets to visually offset the top from the bottom.

With the quiltlets assembled, I could now determine the correct size for the cradled board. The shuttle determined the width, and the placement of the elements dictated the length. The cut size of the background fabric is determined by the size of the cradled board (see page 85).

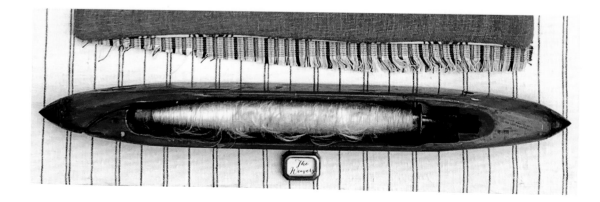

I applied a thin layer of glue to the board with an old credit card used as a squeegee. I smoothed the background fabric over the board, working from the center out to the edges, and allowed it to dry. Once it was dry, I applied glue to the board edges and glued the fabric along the sides up to, but not including, the corners. I glued the remaining fabric to the back edges of the board—again up to, but not including, the corners.

I folded the fabric at each corner and mitered it, then trimmed off the excess. Then I glued the fabric at each corner.

I added a third fabric to offset the quilt from the background fabric covering the board. I adhered the quilt layers to the board with 4 strips of carpet tape. These will hold them in place and allows for future removal if necessary. I glued the shuttle in place with wood glue using C-clamps to secure it while the glue dried and cured overnight. (Cardboard was placed on the shuttle to protect it from the clamps). I glued on the small brass frame as the final touch.

Detail of mitered corner

Calculating Fabric Size for Cradled Board

Cradled boards typically come in 3 depths: ⅞″, 1½″, and 2″. I prefer the 1½″ depth because it gives more visual weight and importance to the art.

The front of the board measured 14″ × 18″. Each side is 1½″, so I added 3″ to my measurements for the sides. The back edge measured ¾″. I added an additional 1″ on each edge (2″ total), to allow for the fabric to be folded over and glued to that area.

Total size of fabric to cover board: 14 + 3 + 2 = 19, and 18 + 3 + 2 = 23. The fabric was cut 19″ × 23″.

Photographing History

As you know by now, the history of photography, tintypes, and old photographs is a passion of mine. Imagine my delight when I discovered the Liljenquist Family Collection of Civil War Photographs online at the Library of Congress. For me, this collection of photographs brought the Civil War out of the history books and onto the faces of the people who lived through it. I have a personal interest in this part of our American history, not because of relatives who fought in the war (there were none), but because I have spent my life surrounded by places connected to the war. I know the towns and battlefields, the hospitals, monuments, government buildings, and Arlington cemetery, one of the first national cemeteries, created as a result of that war. It is located across the Potomac River from Washington, D.C., and is where my parents are buried.

For most of my life I was aware of, but not really interested in, the history of this area I call home. Now, with the wisdom of age and the time to indulge, I search for photographs to show and stories to tell, to inform and bring light to the individuals that were here before me.

Photographing History was created to honor the early photographers who were the first to photograph history in the making.

Prominent early photographers Timothy H. O'Sullivan (L) and Alexander Gardner (R)
with samples of a photo TAP-transferred onto gray satin (to mimic tintypes)
and white cotton. I decided on the white fabric for this quilt.

Method

To create the background fabric, I edited digital downloads of antique photographs and set them into a repeating grid using Photoshop. I uploaded the design to Spoonflower and had it printed on cotton. To create a tintype appearance, I fused black chiffon to the fabric. I quilted the fabric onto thin batting following the lines of the grid images. This became my collage base.

I enlarged photographs of prominent Civil War photographers Matthew Brady and Alexander Gardner, as well as a group of traveling photographers. I edited the photos and applied a color filter to give them a warm hue.

Some early studios offered the option of adding hand coloring to their portraits. I selected 3 such portraits and edited them, along with 2 additional ones, to be framed. Their dimensionality, variety, touch of color, and scattered appearance break up the static background and further add to the story by re-creating an actual portrait you could hold in your hand.

The addition of the gray satin fabric and the black-and-white ribbon and paper behind the enlarged photographs helps to visually move them forward from the background, add variety, heighten contrast, and echo the repetition in the background.

A section of the background grid

I chose black-and-white fabric with a strong, but not competing, contrast and repeated diagonal pattern to serve as backing and border. The quilt has a package-fold finish (page 58). I folded the edges of the quilted top inward to the back. Then I placed the top onto the batting and backing sandwich, and used a zigzag stitch to attach it to the backing. This double-batted top layer created a wonderful raised effect for the quilt, contrasting it with the recessed frame of the border. I attached the tintype frames with thread and beads, then glued the gem tintypes onto the Brady photo as the final touch.

BRADY
The Photographer
returned from
Bull Run
Wash. D.C.
No 238

PICTURE GALLERY.
PHOTOGRAPHS

Clare Murray Adams

Life is but a Dream ❦ 40˝ × 19´˝

Photo by Clare Murray Adams

Clare's quilt was inspired by a photograph she took while traveling in Ukraine a number of years ago. She fell in love with the energy expressed in the clay figures made by children at a school she visited. Their open and uninhibited expressions led to the idea of them singing the song "Row, Row, Row Your Boat" as a round.

"The original photograph was black and white. I manipulated it in Photoshop and then had Spoonflower print it on cotton fabric in color, as well as on a sheer fabric. The cotton fabric became the base of the quilt top, while the sheer and extra prints on cotton became the appliqué parts. It is primarily hand appliqué and quilted with embroidery.

The words of the song were printed on the computer, then onto Dass Classic Transfer Film and transferred to the sheer organza three times so they could be layered just as the singing is layered when people sing a song in a round.

The appliqué work is mostly hand done, as is the quilting with lots of French knots and some embellishments."—*Clare*

Katherine Stewart Wilson

Grandma's Hands ❦ 21½″ × 27″

Katherine's grandmother, Katherine Jean Queen Maddox, was born in 1901 and lived during a time of limited opportunities for Black women. She worked as a domestic but wanted an existence qualitatively different from the one that had been scripted for her.

In her grandmother's belongings, Katherine found a 1935 letter of reference and her grandmother's business card, marking the start of her journey as an entrepreneur when she opened her own laundry. Katherine portrays her memories of the blue and white dress shirts of her grandma's clients—her grandmother's hands washing the shirts, hanging them to dry for that fresh-air smell, the hand ironing, and folding them to perfection before placing them in laundry baskets to be picked up. This quilt honors Grandma Katherine, who chose possibilities rather than limitations and dared to map her own life.

"For this quilt, I used assorted re-purposed men's cotton dress shirts, commercial cotton print fabrics, African batiks, velvet and polyester scraps and remnants, white cotton fabric, quilt batting and backing, fusible interfacing, stabilizer, painted Lutradur, TAP Transfer Artist Paper, digital or scanned family photos, copyright-free images, a fine-point fabric marking pen, flat thread, ribbon, buttons, and mini wood clothespins. With all the elements prepared for assembly, I created collages representing the laundry."—*Katherine*

Photo by C&T Publishing

KATHERINE'S HAND LAUNDRY

Phone SO 3-0280

ALL TYPES OF LAUNDRY WORK

First Class Work — Prompt Service

51 Church Street   South Orange, N. J.

Linda Trenholm

A Book, A Letter, A Garden and A Girl ❦ *22˝ × 22˝*

Linda began this decorative pillow cover project by laying out a story composed of four anchors to build the design around: a beautiful line drawing of a young girl; an old, tattered math book cover; a handwritten love letter in a foreign language; and a line drawing of a vase of flowers. As she pieced them together with floral-print linens, lace, and fabrics the story began to emerge—*A young woman from a foreign country sets out to teach on a faraway estate, leaving home for the first time. She spends her free time in the vast country gardens dreaming of home while reading love letters from someone she left behind.* Each square of fabric is connected by stitches that weave like a vine to the next block, much like a colorful country garden.

"Inkjet prints of the girl and the floral arrangement were printed onto TAP paper. These images were black-and-white outlines with a cream background. Once printed, the color was gently added with Prismacolor pencils and water-based markers onto the TAP image. Several layers were needed to give a boost to the color. The images were then transferred to cream-colored cotton fabric to create a brighter image. Images were adhered with a light layer of diluted white glue onto the base fabric and reinforced with stitching and/or embroidery."—*Linda*

Photo by C&T Publishing

Beverly Y. Smith

Under Grace ❦ 51″ × 66″

Beverly's concepts and inspirations are derived from books, vintage family photographs, and ancestral research. Her quilt was inspired by her great-cousin, Israel Jackson, who passed away at the pulpit in the historic Grace AME Zion Church in Charlotte, North Carolina, in 1945. Today, Beverly has an art studio set up in the very sanctuary where her relative preached for the two years before his death.

Beverly chooses to express herself through quilts because of their symbolic dimensions and implied spiritual connection between the seen and unseen. Her process uses vintage fabrics paired with her original graphite portrait drawings, embroidery, machine and hand piecing, quilting, and transferred images.

"I used graphite-drawn portraits, vintage lace, feed sacks, a patchwork quilt, embroidery thread, and transferred photographs.

The photographs come from my family's photo album. They date back as far as the 1870s. Mentioned in order: my great-grandmother, Nancy; my aunt, Sarah, holding my brother, Ezekiel, who passed away three months after this photo; and my cousin, Israel Jackson.

The photographs were copied onto TAP Transfer Artist Paper using an inkjet printer. The TAP image was ironed on top of quilted fabric, then the backing of the transfer paper was peeled off."—*Beverly*

Photo by Dan Ormsby

Judy V. Gula

Birdwatching ❧ 14″ × 17″

Judy spends time in Sarasota, Florida, every year. It is there that she found a whole new world of birds. Although she does not claim to be a professional birder, she is delighted and inspired by birds in flight and their striking color combinations.

"I used TAP transfer, a hand-dyed-fabric base, fabric paper, Kraft-tex (from C&T Publishing), and embellishments."—*Judy*

Photo by Kyle Gula

Lorie McCown

Remembrance ❧ 33˝ × 45˝

This quilt was the first one Lorie made after she lost her parents. It is meant to be raw and wrinkled, like old memories and the raw edges of emotions.

"I used recycled household textiles, photo printing on silk organza, and hand stitching."—*Lorie*

Photo by C&T Publishing

Wen Redmond

Shared Remembered Moment ❧ 8½″ × 9″

A memory of that fall day when you came

with me on a walk through the woods.

Naturally we got lost. We continued and found an old abandoned

shack of a garage, roof partially caved in and a jeep, left to rust, covered in leaves.

Sharing our delight, we both took many photos of it.—Wen Redmond

Wen never thought she would use those photos, but this one spoke to her.

"I wanted a surface that was somewhat distressed. I used cotton duck and added torn strips of more cotton duck, sewn down with a wobbly stitching line. I was curious to see how the TAP transfer would work on a surface with lots of texture. The photo of the jeep was perfect. After the transfer, and before it cooled completely, I lifted up some of the edges of the strips, so they would come away from the background. I adhered torn sections of old dress patterns inside and allowed them to peek out. I have tons of them from prior sewing days.

I painted an old, found quilt square with white gesso for the mount. But then I flipped it over and liked the back better. So I mounted the transferred work onto the reverse side of the quilt square, which could be yet another story, of how the quilt movement spoke to me back in the 1970s."—*Wen*

Photo by C&T Publishing

Christine Vinh

A Quiet Oasis ❦ 18″ × 21″

During the pandemic, Christine took many solo walks in nearby Washington, D.C. The Smithsonian Gardens were a frequent starting place, and the route always included a walk through the Mary Livingston Ripley Garden, a small informal garden next to the Arts and Industries Building. The garden was a source of calm and inspiration during her walks. The photos Christine chose for this piece focused on the birdhouse in the center of the garden during the changing seasons.

"My piece includes a collage of my images using a variety of photo manipulation and printing techniques, including Transfer Artist Paper, printing on organza, and printing on cotton sateen. The various images were fused and then machine quilted and embellished with hand stitching."—*Christine*

Photo by Christine Vinh

Margaret Abramshe

Thin Man ✻ 30˝ × 33˝

Thin Man is a portrait of Margaret's paternal grandfather in the last year of his life. He lived in Hollywood, California. The title comes from the *Thin Man* movie series filmed near his house, starring William Powell as detective Nick Charles. Margaret's quilts are often based on old family photographs and current ones she has taken.

"The quilt is a combination of two completed quilts. Both quilts include altered photographs, enlarged, printed commercially on fabric, then glazed with layers of water-soluble paints. The process allows for the printed image to be altered to improve the overall composition. The surface is further embellished with drawing and stitched with contour drawing and surface patterns, with free-motion machine quilting using colored thread over the entire surface. The background areas were removed from the first quilt, and then further cut into pieces that were arranged around the figure in the second quilt to form an irregular frame. A painted organic shape was the final touch."—*Margaret*

Photo by Margaret Abramshe

Michelle Umlauf

The Chickadee ❀ 17¼″ × 23¼″

When Michelle lived on Birdsong Way, she noticed that as soon as she stepped outside, she would hear a bird sing a two-note song. She always returned the song, and a two-note conversation would ensue between the two. After moving away, Michelle would still hear those same two notes whenever she went outside. One day, she set out to read into the message she was receiving and started looking for signs. The letter *Y* kept popping up. "Who do I know has a name that begins with the letter Y?" she asked herself. She did a vivid rewind to her childhood, when her family lived on the same farm as her grandparents, where her grandmother enjoyed sitting on her porch by her flower garden. When she would see Michelle outside playing, she would call from afar, "Yoo-hoo," and Michelle would gleefully sing the tune back. As soon as she made that connection, she cried tears of joy. She doesn't hear that bird as much anymore, but when she does, she knows it's her grandmother's way of saying "I love you." Upon creating this quilt, she discovered that the bird that sings "yoo-hoo" is the chickadee.

"I found a picture of a chickadee and printed it onto a piece of Transfer Artist Paper. I transferred it onto a piece of linen that I probably acquired from my grandmother's stash.

The foundation for the front of this quilt is cotton duck and thread. I created the binding using a serger wave stitch (exclusive to some Baby Lock sergers) and 12-wt. cotton thread and blendable thread. The three-dimensional thread-lace leaves were stitched with 40-wt. rayon thread and painted to give them more dimension. To make this piece more personal, I wrote the words and drew the musical lines, and took a picture with my phone. I transferred the photos to my machine and manipulated and converted them into embroidery stitches (on a Baby Lock Solaris). I machine embroidered the words *Yoo Hoo* and added quilting in IQ Designer using a built-in motif and embroidered onto cotton fabric."—*Michelle*

Photo by C&T Publishing

Yoo Hoo

Everytime I hear a chickadee

I know it's singing

a special song

just for me.

"Yoo-Hoo" means

I love you, Nanny.

Bobbi Baugh

Looking Below the Surface ❦ 33″ × 43″

This work is both a preservation and an exploration of a place. A pond on a family member's farm in North Georgia is the setting. Bobbi remembers being there, enjoying the place, and becoming contemplative as she looked at the shadows and ripples in the water. Her quilt is the visual story of her wondering about what life there was, at that moment, that she could not see.

"I created the right half of the quilt with hand-printed, layered tissue paper to give a voice to that unseen life. The photo portion preserves the place as I saw it. The hand-printed portion explores what was invisible in the photo. I added a gel-medium transfer of a laser color copy onto muslin. I enlarged the original photo to the final size in Photoshop Elements and tiled for output on individual 11″ × 17″ sheets. I pieced together the copies with tape to make one large paper copy and transferred it onto a single piece of muslin, which I machine quilted."—*Bobbi*

Photo by Bobbi Baugh

Suzanne Coley

The Masks We Wear ❦ 32″ × 45″

This is an original design inspired by Suzanne's lifelong passion for classic literature and historical textiles. The main fabric is from curtains that once hung in someone's living room. The backing fabric was formerly a sheet that dressed a bed. The hand-dyed binding used to be a dress. She purchased these repurposed, everyday, utilitarian textiles at her local thrift store. By transforming them into a work of art, Suzanne offers a more poetic reading of Shakespeare's Sonnet 116 and gives this piece additional layers of story and meaning.

"I cut, painted, and sewed repurposed clothing, upholstery fabric, bed linens, and grosgrain ribbon. I created silkscreens, adding emulsion and burning them before using them to print the text (Shakespeare's Sonnet 116, in the public domain). I used a hand-cut linoleum block to stamp images. I repurposed a butterfly fabric from a thrift store to appliqué and embroider the butterfly."—*Suzanne*

Photo by C&T Publishing

Sonnet CXVI

Let me not to the marriage of true minds
Admit impediments. Love is not love
Which alters when it alteration finds
Or bends with the remover to remove:
O no! it is an ever-fixed mark
That looks on tempests and is never shaken;
It is the star to every wand'ring bark,
Whose worth's unknown, although his height be taken.
Love's not Time's fool, though rosy lips and cheeks
Within his bending sickle's compass come;
Love alters not with his brief hours and weeks,
But bears it out even to the edge of doom.
If this be error and upon me prov'd,
I never writ, nor no man ever lov'd.

Whitney Dahlberg

Reflections ❊ 18″ × 22″

What people see of us on the outside is rarely reflective of the kaleidoscope of imagination, emotions, and experiences of our inner worlds. Whitney's inspiration for this piece stems from her thoughts about the different roles people play throughout various relationships in their lives. These roles can range from prescribed labels such as sister, wife, daughter, or friend to the relational archetypes we embody: the child, the protector, the hero, the victim, the creator. What shows is only a tiny window into that inner world.

"I took the images on my phone during a morning walk in my neighborhood. I altered them in a pencil-sketch phone app, printed them onto TAP, and transferred them onto cotton. I hand painted the images using Gelatos pigment sticks with a brush. Other materials include quilting cotton, embroidery floss, and hand-painted organza."—*Whitney*

Photo by C&T Publishing

Susan Brubaker Knapp

The Graduate ❦ 23½″ × 25″

This quilt features a photograph of Susan's daughter, Lea, at her college graduation dinner celebration. Susan loves how joyful this piece is, bringing back so many sweet memories of that evening.

"I digitally manipulated a photo and had it printed on fabric by Spoonflower. I pieced it with other fabrics, including some hand-dyed ones, and wrote on it, by hand, with a purple pigment marker. I also used an antique Belgian napkin from a neighbor that I paint-dyed bright orange. After piecing the quilt together, I painted the black circles on top and free-motion machine quilted it. Other materials include cotton fabric, acrylic textile paint, cotton batting, and cotton backing."—*Susan*

Anne Sonner

My Grandmothers ❦ 39″ × 39″

This quilt is a tribute to Anne's maternal and paternal grandmothers, who both died before she was born. She tells their stories through photos and words: their childhoods, careers, marriages, children, and heartbreaks. Fun photos include Edith's booklet from the *Lusitania*, on which she traveled to Europe in 1912, and Carrie driving a Model T Ford while working as a traveling nurse. Images of Anne's four great-grandmothers look on from the hexagon rosettes.

"I printed family photos onto fabric. Then I added appliqué by hand and machine. I rust-dyed and indigo-dyed (with the shibori technique) antique cotton damask napkins, and embroidered words. Other materials include vintage laces, textiles, and buttons."—*Anne*

Photo by David Sonner

My Grandmothers

Carolyn
Scott
Rowland

1889 ~ 1950

Al Krueger

Muscle Man ✸ 54″ × 53″

Al says, "I'd do anything to look like that … except diet and exercise." This quilt embodies his heartfelt desire to look muscular and buff, countered by his real reluctance to do the actual work required to attain that goal. Sound familiar?

"I used a stock image from Depositphotos for the muscle man and then electronically pasted my head onto the body using Photoshop, adding the text, "I'd Do Anything …,' also using Photoshop. I sent the completed black-and-white image to a fabric printing service (Spoonflower) and had it transferred to organic cotton sateen. I stabilized it with fusible interfacing and then enhanced the lines and texture of the photo collage with hand embroidery. I used a trapunto technique to emphasize the bulging muscles of the figure. I backed the head and body with thick wool batting and then outlined it with free-motion stitching. I trimmed away the excess batting outside the stitching lines. I layered backing, thin cotton batting, and the top, and free-motion quilted it. I used dense quilting outside of the figure to emphasize the bulges. The quilt was traditionally bound."—*Al*

Photo by Lausch Photography

I'd do anything to look like that...

Except DIET and EXERCISE

Patty Kennedy-Zafred

Catch & Release ⚜ 44″ × 41″

Watching her son and his wife fly fish, waist-high in a rippling stream or perched on the edge of a boat, is magical to Patty. The quietness of the sport, coupled with the refined movements of casting, is a pleasure to witness. The time-honored practice of catch-and-release requires careful handling and quick action, helping to conserve the fish population and natural habitat. Her son also ties his own flies, which are true works of art, often using Sulky metallic silver threads familiar to many stitchers. Favorite spots to cast include their local Charleston coastal marshes and secluded spots in North Carolina. For Patty, creating this quilt, using photos her son and daughter-in-law took, is a remembrance of these memories and a lasting gift for the entire family to share. (Patty shared that Spoonflower stated that its process would not withstand dyeing. It's a good tip to have.)

"Fabric on Demand is the only print-on-demand company that utilizes a dye print process that never fades and can withstand the harsh chemicals of Procion dye. I had the photos printed in black and white, did multiple dye techniques (shibori, rope, etc.) and overdyed the pieces, and they never faded. I used cotton fabric, Procion MX dyes, and cotton batting; digital fiber reactive dye-printed images, overdyed multiple times; hand-dyed fabric using shibori and resist techniques; and machine piecing and quilting."—*Patty*

Photo by Larry Berman

Gina Louthian-Stanley
Navigating ❧ 13½″ × 20″

Birds have fascinated Gina all of her life. As a matter of fact, the first word she uttered was "bird." To this day Gina is an avid bird-watcher and gardener. The flowers and organic shapes are indicative of the native plants she grows in her garden for pollinators and birds. This piece is reflective of her memory of watching the birds from her parents' living room window. She has always been intrigued by how birds navigate and move throughout nature.

"I used an old floral shirt for the base and Liquitex paint markers and gel pens (for fine lines) to enhance the colors by painting some of the flowers. Then I added the bird image, which was transferred using TAP (which I love), to another piece of fabric. Using my free-motion foot, I used stitches to create subtle navigational lines. The navigational map was printed by running painted canvas fabric through a laser printer. I added painted fabrics and some hand stitching to several areas to complete the piece. The blue circle is meaningful to me because I'm always making a reference to how I navigate in life. I ask myself, for instance, 'How will I navigate coping with a family member's illness? How can I work full time and still teach art classes and still create?' Sometimes navigating is not a straight line … however, I find life is cyclic. Birds have always seemed to highlight my art, plus, they are great navigators!"—*Gina*

Photo by C&T Publishing

Contributors

MARGARET ABRAMSHE

margaretabramshe.com

IG: @abramshe_textilearts

CLARE MURRAY ADAMS

claremurrayadams.com

IG: @claremurrayadams

BOBBI BAUGH

bobbibaughstudio.com

IG: @bobbibaughart

FB: bobbibaughart

SUZANNE COLEY

suzannecoley.com

IG: @baltimoresonnets

WHITNEY DAHLBERG

whitneydahlberg.com

IG: @the_meditative_stitcher

KIM EICHLER-MESSMER

kimemquilts.com

IG: @kimemquilts

JUDY V. GULA

artisticartifacts.com

IG: @artistic_artifacts

FB: ArtisticArtifacts

PATTY KENNEDY-ZAFRED

pattykz.com

IG: @pattykz1

FB: Patty Kennedy-Zafred

SUSAN BRUBAKER KNAPP

susanbrubakerknapp.com

AL KRUEGER

IG: @akrubear

GINA LOUTHIAN-STANLEY

ginalouthian-stanleyartist.com

IG: @ginalouthianstanleyartist

LORI MCCOWN

loriemccown.com

SUSAN L. PRICE

IG: @susanprice24 and @pgfiber2art

FB: Susan Price and PGFiber2Art

WEN REDMOND

wenredmond.com

IG: @wenredmond

BEVERLY Y. SMITH

beverlyysmithart.com

IG: @quiltbev

ANNE SONNER

annesonnerquilts.wordpress.com

LINDA TRENHOLM

lindytrenholm.com

IG: @lindy_trenholm

MICHELLE UMLAUF

sewingmachineartistry.com

FB: Sewing Machine Artistry

CHRISTINE VINH

FB: Stitchesnquilts

KATHERINE STEWART WILSON

FB: Katherine Stewart Wilson

NANETTE S. ZELLER

NanetteSewZ.com

Resources

Photo Sources

Boston College Libraries, "Finding Images": libguides.bc.edu/findingimages/Copyright

Creative Commons: commons.wikimedia.org/wiki/Commons:Free_media_resources/Photography
Indexes over 300 million images from multiple image collections, including works from museums, photos from Flickr, and many more. All of the indexed images are in the public domain and released under Creative Commons licenses, meaning the images are generally free to use in a noncommercial setting.

Flickr.com

Not all images are copyright free.

Getty Open Content Image Collection:
The Getty makes available, without charge, more than 10,000 images from the J. Paul Getty Museum and the Getty Research Institute in its Open Content Program. The Getty holds the rights to these images, or they are in the public domain and can be used for any purpose. No permission is required.

Google Image:
Searchable by text or image. Allows searches filtered by usage rights (educational purposes, publishing, etc.).

Library of Congress, "Health Sciences and Medicine" research guide: guides.loc.gov/science-images-and-videos/health-sciences

Library of Congress: loc.gov

The Public Domain Review: publicdomainreview.org

U.S. National Archives and Records Administration

Digital Public Library of America: Limited access without an account.

Wikimedia Commons Images: commons.wikimedia.org

The following sites offer free, copyright-free, contemporary images for download. Some will ask that you provide attribution to the photographer when used.

Burst: burst.shopify.com

Gratisography: gratisography.com

Life of Pix: lifeofpix.com

Pexels: pexels.com

Pixabay: pixabay.com

Realistic Shots: realisticshots.com

StockSnap: stocksnap.io

Unsplash: unsplash.com

Photos for Purchase

Clancy's Classics: ebay.com/str/clancysclassics
Vintage photographs 1860–1960s.

Lesley Riley: lesleyriley.com
Vintage photos ready to print on fabric or TAP. Instant downloads.

Helpful Information and Photo Resources

Copyrightlaws.com, "6 Best Practices for Legally Using Google Images": copyrightlaws.com/copyright-tips-legally-using-google-images/

Nations Photo Lab, "Pixel Chart": nationsphotolab.com/pixelchart.aspx
A user-friendly chart equating pixels to printable size.

Posterizer: posterizer.online
Tile and print an image in sections.

TinEye, tineye.com:
Reverse image search.

Suppliers

Search for the following at google.com.

BERNINA

InkAid

Jacquard Inkjet Printable Fabric

Amazon

Jacquard Products (cyanotype and Solarfast)

Dharma Trading

Talasonline.com

About the Author

Lesley Riley never intended to be a full-time, professional artist. She just followed her passion in the small blocks of time she carved out while raising six children. Now, as an internationally known instructor and multimedia artist, Lesley creates quilts, mixed and digital media, paintings, and botanical prints. In 1999, she turned her initial passion for fabric, photos, color, and the written word into a dream occu*passion* that continues to delight and inspire creatives and art lovers everywhere. A quilter since 1971, Lesley has a wealth of knowledge in using color and pattern to create innovative art quilts and fabric collage. Her interest is in creating work that references the historical by bringing it into a personal and contemporary context.

Photo by Rebecca Carpenter

Lesley has written several books and articles, has been a guest on several episodes of *Quilting Arts TV,* was profiled on *The Quilt Show,* was a BERNINA Ambassador, and is an educator for Golden Artist Colors. Her line of botanical-inspired fabric is licensed with Northcott Fabrics. As a sought-after workshop instructor, Lesley focuses on motivating, inspiring, and empowering beginning and seasoned artists and quilters to take their creative life into their own hands by encouraging students to take risks, think outside the box, and break rules. Her emphasis is on understanding composition and using techniques and materials to discover and enhance the maker's own creativity and unique voice.

WEBSITE: lesleyriley.com

INSTAGRAM: @lrileyart

FACEBOOK: /lesley.riley.art

PINTEREST: /lesleyriley

Creativity abounds in an empty nest she shares with her high school–sweetheart husband on a mountaintop in Cascade, Maryland. You'll find Lesley in her upstairs and down, indoor and outdoor studios from sunup to sundown unless, of course, any of her sixteen grandchildren come to visit.

In the end, we'll all become stories.
— MARGARET ATWOOD —